GW00778278

the invention of chic
thérèse bonney and paris moderne

lisa schlansker kolosek

with 186 illustrations

Thames & Hudson

Photographs pages 1–5. Page 1: Stag's head door pulls in plated metal from the Rose Valois millinery shop (18, rue Royale), designed by Billard & Callet. This typical Art Deco motif was carried throughout the interior. Pages 2–3: "Chrysanthème" pressed-glass table service designed by André Hunebelle, ca. 1930, a popular pattern often used in advertisements for Hunebelle's shop on the avenue Victor-Emmanuel-III. This page: Art Deco salon designed by Jules-Emile Leleu, "one of the outstanding decorators of present day Paris," according to Bonney. "Geometry is still the guiding spirit of the modern French room."

Any copy of this book issued by the publisher as a paperback is sold subject to the condition that it shall not by way of trade or otherwise be lent, resold, hired out or otherwise circulated without the publisher's prior consent in any form of binding or cover other than that in which it is published and without a similar condition including these words being imposed on a subsequent purchaser.

First published in the United Kingdom in 2002 by Thames & Hudson Ltd, 181A High Holborn, London WC1V 7QX

www.thamesandhudson.com

© 2002 Smithsonian Institution

All Rights Reserved. No part of this publication may be reproduced or transmitted in any form or by any means, electronic or mechanical, including photocopy, recording or any other information storage and retrieval system, without prior permission in writing from the publisher.

British Library Cataloguing-in-Publication Data A catalogue record for this book is available from the British Library

ISBN 0-500-510962

Printed and bound in Hong Kong by C&C Offset

contents

_foreword

Cooper-Hewitt, National Design Museum holds an extraordinary archive of work by Thérèse Bonney, an important photographer of modern architecture and design in 1920s and 1930s France. With more than 4,000 photos, it is a thorough and unique resource for understanding how modern design as we know it came to be defined. Bonney photographed work by people who became legendary—such as Le Corbusier, Charlotte Perriand, and Robert Mallet-Stevens, to name just a few—as well as by others less well known. She photographed furniture that is still being manufactured now, eighty years later, and window displays that of course were never intended to stand the test of time and were dismantled after only a week or two. She photographed people's homes, interiors of stores, world's fairs, and ocean liners. It is perhaps her photos of the ephemeral and lesser known that are most valuable to historians and design enthusiasts today. It is through these images that we see the many varied strains of early modern design—from the austere to the ostentatious, and everything in between.

Bonney's photos provide a fuller knowledge of design's evolution, and I am pleased to present this diverse selection of them. Lisa Schlansker Kolosek's book began as a thesis in the Museum's Masters Program in the History of Decorative Arts, which is offered in association with Parsons School of Design, a division of New School University, and The Smithsonian Associates in Washington, DC. Supplemented with years of additional research and travel, her thesis grew into the current volume. I thank Lisa, the staff of Thames & Hudson, and everyone at Cooper-Hewitt, National Design Museum for their hard work in creating this beautiful book.

Paul Warwick Thompson, Director

Cooper-Hewitt, National Design Museum, Smithsonian Institution

Wallpaper designed by Eric Bagge

for Desfosse-Karth. Thérèse Bonney captured modern design in all its forms and all its scales—from architecture and installations at world's fairs to small decorative objects. Bagge's graphic wallpaper design was rendered in sumptuous materials: silk fabric embossed onto opaque paper.

_introduction

"An American—Witness of Her Time:" that was the fitting title for a planned—though sadly never realized—retrospective of the remarkable life of M. Thérèse Bonney (1894–1978), photojournalist, author, scholar, curator, collector, and humanitarian. She began working in photojournalism in postwar Paris after a brilliant academic career that culminated in a Ph.D. from the Sorbonne. In the early 1920s, she founded the first American illustrated press service in Europe, which went on to supply photographs of modern French design and architecture to more than twenty countries worldwide. Thérèse Bonney and her staff photographers extensively documented the modern design movement in Paris between the two world wars, from the annual salon installations to international expositions, interiors of private homes and public spaces, architecture and the decorative arts. Their work, now housed in an archive at Cooper-Hewitt, National Design Museum in New York, amounts to nothing less than a thorough representation of the period, from sumptuous Art Deco to more purist, functional forms. The Bonney Service existed until the late 1930s, paralleling one of the most socially, culturally, and artistically rich eras in Parisian history.

Bonney's success in a male-dominated business during a world depression was borne of specific personality traits. From those who knew her and from her manuscripts, it is clear that Bonney was tough in both professional and personal matters. She was tenacious and often difficult. A big ego, coupled with remarkable public relations

The villa of couturier Jacques Heim (17, avenue de Madrid, Neuilly-sur-Seine), by Gabriel Guévrékian, 1927–28. OPPOSITE Stair landing with sand-colored walls, tubular railing, porthole window, and marble tiles with a graphic zebra-skin rug. ABOVE Bonney was impressed by the bold modernity of the exterior: "Red bricks pave the garden of the ultra-modern home of Monsieur Jacques Heim at Neuilly…concrete flower boxes add a new note…note unusual architecture of the house itself, in concrete with many terraces enclosed with iron tube railing."

Thérèse Bonney, ca. 1930. Bonney was always savvy about her appearance and wore carefully selected fashions for publicity shots like this one. Unfortunately, it is not known who took this photograph of her.

savvy, made for a kind of obsession with her own celebrity. At the dawn of the media age, she skillfully used her fame to promote her business and professional interests. Most importantly, she was extremely hard working. She made her humble origins a baseline for measuring her later high level of success. From the start of her career in Paris until her death in the late 1970s, she was always involved with several projects at once. She had boundless energy, a curious mind, and a vast range of interests.

Born and raised in the United States, Bonney chose France as her home. Throughout her sixty years there, she continually forged alliances between the two countries. In addition to operating her press service in the 1920s and '30s, Bonney wrote articles on French design and architecture that were published in American journals and newspapers. Her largest written work was a unique series of guidebooks published in 1929 with her sister Louise—beginning with *A Shopping Guide to Paris*, and then two subsequent books, *Buying Antique and Modern Furniture in Paris* and *A Guide to the Restaurants of Paris*.[1] That same year the Bonney sisters published *French Cooking for American Kitchens* and in 1930 its British companion, *French Cooking for English Kitchens*. During the 1930s Thérèse published two more books: *Remember When?*, a photographic chronicle of the Edwardian era, and *The Vatican*. She also organized exhibitions of French art in the United States and undertook public relations work in the U.S. for French artists and designers.

Working in Paris, Bonney focused her enterprise on the United States, where she believed "our offices, our motors, our clothes, reflect modern life" but "our furniture and our homes are of the past."[2] By documenting the modern movement as it developed in Paris and selling her photographs for publication, she also sold modernism itself.

Modernism as it was expressed in Paris in the 1920s had its roots in the Art Nouveau style of the late nineteenth and early twentieth centuries. Art Nouveau, characterized by erotic, attenuated forms derived from nature, developed as a reaction against historicism. It first flourished in France, led by, among others, the architect Hector Guimard, reached its climax at the 1900 Paris Exposition Universelle, and lost favor in the opening decade of the twentieth century. It was interpreted in many other countries including Germany (where it was known as the *Jugendstil*), Austria, Belgium, England, and the United States. Throughout Europe, modernism continued to evolve

during the 1900s and 1910s. By the time Bonney became involved with design photography in the mid-1920s, Parisian design had embraced modernism, a term covering a range of alternative modes—from the relatively ornate Art Deco to a strict machine aesthetic, and gradations in between. Bonney photographed the full spectrum.

Among her earliest ventures in the field was the 1925 Paris Exposition Internationale des Arts Décoratifs et Industriels Modernes, one of the most significant events in the history of French design. The Exposition followed a call to French architects and

The spectacular mirrored bar at Le Boeuf sur le Toit (26, rue de Penthièvre). This famous nightclub adopted its name (meaning "the cow on the roof") from the title of a 1920 pantomime-ballet by writer Jean Cocteau and composer Darius Milhaud. Cocteau, Milhaud, and much of the Parisian avant-garde frequented the club.

Jacques-Emile Ruhlmann and D.I.M. decorators
were two designers highly regarded by Bonney. ABOVE Rosewood
dressing table by Ruhlmann. RIGHT ABOVE State bedroom by
Ruhlmann for the 1928 Salon des Artistes Décorateurs. Bonney
commended the cabinetmaker for linking modernism with French
tradition by repeating "the graceful lines of the past in his furniture of
today," and she considered his work "an exquisite example of
craftsmanship and taste." OPPOSITE Entrance of a private apartment
by D.I.M. The rubber floor and oilcloth upholstery were dark red.

designers to create a new aesthetic free of historical references. It was essentially a calculated attempt by France to regain its leadership position in the decorative arts, a position lost to more industrialized nations in Europe, especially Germany, since the beginning of the century.[3] Art Deco, as it is broadly known today, reached its pinnacle at the 1925 Exposition and was the most widely represented style there. Highly decorative and ornamental, it commonly used expensive and exotic woods and materials (such as shagreen, or sharkskin), and techniques and treatments such as lacquer. It can also be recognized by the application of bold color; abstract geometric, Cubist-inspired forms; geometricized natural forms such as flowers; and exotic motifs borrowed from African and Egyptian art. Born as a national style in France, it was quickly adopted internationally.[4] Leading proponents of Art Deco include French designer and cabinetmaker Jacques-Emile Ruhlmann, Swiss-born designer Jean Dunand, the design firm of Süe et Mare (Compagnie des Arts Français), furniture designer André Groult, interior designer Paul Follot, and artist-designer Clément Rousseau. In Paris, the Art Deco style also flourished in the fine arts and in jewelry, fashion, and graphic design.

Coexisting with the luxury and ornament of Art Deco was another, much more austere avant-garde trend, whose advocates placed contemporary life and industrial production at the center of their practice. At the forefront was Swiss-born architect

Le Corbusier (Charles-Edouard Jeanneret). The 1925 Exposition included an important early example of his work in Paris, the Pavillon de l'Esprit Nouveau, which he erected in collaboration with his cousin Pierre Jeanneret. Designed as a standardized dwelling, it was fitted with modular storage systems and mass-produced furniture such as Thonet's bentwood armchair. Paintings by Le Corbusier and Fernand Léger, inspired by the machine age, hung in the pavilion. Le Corbusier championed purism, rationalism, functionalism, and standardization in design, ideas which were also interpreted by a number of other architects and designers in Paris including Francis Jourdain, architect Robert Mallet-Stevens, architect Georges Djo-Bourgeois, furniture designer Charlotte Perriand (an associate of Le Corbusier), and architect René Herbst. These designers embraced modern materials such as tubular steel and glass; refrain from ornament; clarity and order; restrained, harmonious color schemes; and geometric forms. Furthermore, they believed that modern methods of production should make the highest quality of design available to the masses.

Between these two camps was a broad middle ground. Nonetheless one could often determine the aesthetic and social tendencies of French architects and designers in the interwar years by their membership in one of two powerful exhibition societies: the Société des Artistes Décorateurs, a fairly conservative group, or the Union des Artistes Modernes (UAM), a body of more progressive designers and architects who favored a more functional, unornamented aesthetic. UAM was founded in opposition to the Société in 1929 by members such as Herbst, Mallet-Stevens, Jourdain, Perriand, textile designer Hélène Henry, and furniture designer Eileen Gray. (These groups are discussed in more detail in chapter 3.)

The New York stock market crash in 1929 directly affected the European economy, and ultimately the design industry. As a consequence, by the 1930s, modern French design had begun to slowly evolve away from luxury goods toward more sober forms suitable for serial production. In this development, it was greatly influenced by other modern movements throughout Europe in the first decades of the twentieth century, including those of Germany and Holland, the Soviet Union and Scandinavia. In Germany, modern design had long been firmly rooted in machine production. This principle was first promoted as early as 1907 by the Deutscher Werkbund, an association of artists and manufacturers devoted to improving the quality and

La Semaine à Paris newspaper offices
(26, rue d'Assas), by Robert Mallet-Stevens, ca. 1930.
ABOVE Detail of the building's facade, showing the zinc relief by Joël and Jan Martel that flanked the door. Seven stained-glass windows by Louis Barillet and Jacques Le Chevallier represented the days of the week and various leisure activities.
OPPOSITE Office of the Administrator, by Charlotte Perriand, Le Corbusier, and Pierre Jeanneret. The designers featured tubular steel furniture, including their iconic Grand Confort chair.

Private bar on casters (shown open), designed by renowned modernist silversmith Jean Puiforcat. The combination of polished metal and rosewood was signature Puiforcat. His silver tablewares were often detailed with semiprecious stones and rare woods.

design of German consumer goods, and later by the Bauhaus school of art and design founded in 1919, where the ultimate objective was to train artists and create prototypes for industry.[5] An international program of design was engendered at the Bauhaus by a faculty whose members represented the avant-garde from the Soviet Union, Hungary, Holland, Switzerland, and the United States, in addition to Germany. Other important modern movements that developed simultaneously include Constructivism in the Soviet Union (and Eastern Europe) and De Stijl in Holland, both of which were influenced by Cubism in France.[6] Constructivist design, created by, among others, the versatile Russian artist Aleksandr Rodchenko, was based on socialist theories and a machine aesthetic. Forms were standard, rational, functional or multifunctional, economical, and above all suited to mass-production and the broad needs of society. Color schemes were often restricted to black, white, gray, and red. De Stijl was similarly rational, based on a strict vocabulary of horizontal and vertical lines; abstract, geometric forms; and a color palette of the primary colors red, blue, and yellow in addition to black, white, and gray in order to achieve a harmonious aesthetic reflective of modern life. The most notable De Stijl designers included the architects Theo Van Doesburg, Gerrit Rietveld, and J.J.P. Oud. Modern Scandinavian design made a tangible impact on the international stage in the 1930s, especially in the work of Finnish architect Alvar Aalto. This unique brand of modernism was based on craft traditions and democratic ideals, and, particularly in furniture design, combined natural materials such as birch wood with simple, curvilinear forms. Scandinavian modern design was generally standardized, functional, and affordable, essentially adhering to the principles of the international style being created in Germany, the Soviet Union, and Holland.

The development of modern design in France was closely linked with these movements, especially that of Germany, which fueled them all. Furthermore, there were a number of Parisian designers who worked or trained in these countries in the years leading up to the 1920s and were influenced by the shared principles of rationalization and standardization. Le Corbusier, who became the unofficial leader of the most progressive strain of modern design in France after he settled in Paris in 1919, had worked in Germany in 1910 for architect Peter Behrens, a founding member of the Deutscher Werkbund. He had been part of the international style in design from its inception.

Thérèse Bonney was drawn to what she saw as the beauty of modernism, and was repeatedly quoted as stating that hers were pictures with ideas. Her choices of subject matter, including in her work in fashion and portraiture, carried a proselytizing message. In addition to capturing a democratic cross-section of French design, she wrote captions for her photos that consistently emphasized modernism. Alongside a photograph of a ceramic plate designed by French ceramist and glassware designer Marcel Goupy, for example, she wrote: "Monogram of the modern plate becomes part

Living room designed by Pierre-Paul Montagnac, with a gilded wooden screen by Jean Dunand in the far right corner. Montagnac's neutral shell consists of walls covered with gray fabric and gray wood panels, an off-white ceiling, and a brown and cream carpet by Ivan Da Silva-Bruhns. Set within is dark polished wooden furniture upholstered in brown satin and curtains of orange silk and brown velour.

Avant-garde designer Jean Prouvé
created these metal and opaque glass doors for a villa
designed by architect Robert Mallet-Stevens. A friend and
collaborator of Mallet-Stevens, Prouvé contributed to several
of his commissions, including the rue Mallet-Stevens.

of the decorative design…placing of monogram allows for much freedom of choice… sometimes in center, sometimes to one side, and occasionally on extreme edge of plate…faïence services much in vogue in Paris of today."[7] She said herself that her captions served to "explain and amplify the story told by the picture." In most cases, they did so by relating the subject to some aspect of contemporary Parisian life.[8]

This book covers Bonney's first twenty years in Paris—her life and career—and the important body of work she created during that time. With the onset of World War II, Thérèse Bonney's lens shifted from architecture and design to the conflict at hand, and she never returned to her original subject matter. However, she was keenly aware of the documentary importance of her body of work. Bonney knew she had witnessed one of the most significant moments in the history of design, architecture, and fashion in France. Because of this, she elected to offer her collection to a museum rather than a private dealer. "Though the offer you make…is considerably less than is offered me here [in Paris], I am accepting it because I would like to have the Cooper Union Museum have them, because I believe that they are of importance for a Reference Library."[9] Thus today, Cooper-Hewitt, National Design Museum (successor to the Cooper Union Museum) is the sole repository in the United States of Bonney's photographs of architecture and design. This unique documentary collection contains more than four thousand, 8" x 10" (20 x 25 cm) black and white prints that were taken either by Bonney herself (or her staff photographers) or by other photographers and purchased by Bonney.[10] The photographs at Cooper-Hewitt document 1920s and '30s Parisian domestic and commercial architecture and interiors, storefronts and window displays, exposition and salon installations, architectural elements, furniture, glass, ceramics, textiles, metalwork, lighting, jewelry, costume, toys, bookbinding, graphic art, and mannequins. They also include, though to a far lesser extent, photographs of architecture and decorative arts taken in Germany, Sweden, Holland, and rural France.

Although not all of the photographs in the Bonney collection were shot by her, she alone compiled them, so they can be taken to represent her vision of the era. However, in selecting images to include in this volume, an effort was made to use prints from the Bonney Service and those that retained her original captions. Furthermore, because it is nearly impossible to determine which photographs were taken by Bonney's own hand, all images throughout this book will be referred to as hers, as they would have

Monogrammed faïence dinner plate by Marcel Goupy, with red geometric motifs. This and other Goupy designs were sold through the glass and ceramic boutique Maison Georges Rouard (34, avenue de l'Opéra), which also carried small works by Jean Dunand, silversmith Jean Puiforcat, and glass designer Henri Navarre.

Tearoom designed by Louis Sognot for Primavera, the design atelier of the department store Au Printemps. This photograph was published in American *Vogue*, 14 September 1929, when the space was exhibited at the 1929 Salon des Artistes Décorateurs.

been if supplied through her press service. (Regrettably, the names of the photographers she employed are now lost.) With rare exceptions, none of the Bonney images at Cooper-Hewitt are labeled with original dates. Some—those of salon installations, international exhibitions, and the work of several notable architects and designers—can be dated from other sources; the remainder are presumed to have been taken between 1925 and 1935.

A small percentage of the photos used in this book have been borrowed from other institutions in order to complete the picture of Thérèse Bonney's work during these years, including photographs from the 1937 Paris Exposition Internationale des Arts et Techniques dans la Vie Moderne, and images of the notable inhabitants of Paris including artists, designers, and couturières, for which the Bonney Service was well known, but which do not form part of the Cooper-Hewitt collection.

Thérèse Bonney's life and work are a rich source for understanding the twentieth century. *The Invention of Chic* focuses specifically on how she documented modern Parisian design and architecture during the creative ferment of the 1920s and '30s. Chapter 1 describes her background and presents the city that she encountered when she moved to Paris in 1919. Chapter 2 examines her press service and her documentation of fashion, beauty, and luxury goods, as well as her friendships and her growing celebrity in the French and American press. Chapter 3 presents many of the venues where she captured the modern movement and the architects, designers, and decorators who fueled it. It looks in detail at Bonney's documentation of the 1937 Paris Exposition, the last significant example of her work in design, and the unique role she assumed in interpreting the fair for an American audience. Chapter 4 explores her efforts to promote the modern movement in the United States through popular channels such as leading newspapers, journals, and books. The United States lacked an avant-garde design world of its own in the early twentieth century; modernism needed a press agent. Thérèse Bonney proved to be just the person.

Greyhound sculpture by Henri Bouchard
in a strikingly Art Deco style for the Sèvres porcelain factory. Thérèse Bonney described Bouchard as "one of the present-day artists who has been called upon by famous *porcelaine* factory at Sèvres to help in the modernization of its formula."

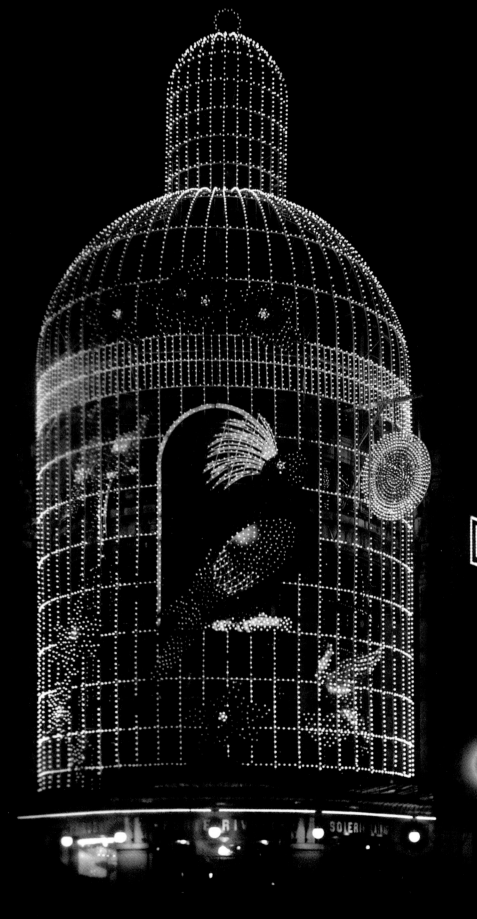

1_paris between the wars

Mabel Thérèse Bonney was born in Syracuse, New York, on 15 July 1894, to Addie Robie and Anthony LeRoy Bonney. Both her parents worked, Anthony Bonney as an electrician and Addie Bonney as a bank clerk and bookkeeper. Thérèse's only sibling, Louise Emily Bonney, had been born five years earlier, in February 1889. Although the families of both parents had lived in New York state for several generations, the Bonneys moved to northern California at the turn of the century. They first went to Sacramento, as early as 1903, and then on to Oakland.

Between 1909 and 1913, Bonney attended the College of the Holy Names in Oakland, a small Roman Catholic school where she was one of a graduating class of only seven.[1] During these formative years some of her most fundamental principles and interests developed. Her indefatigable work ethic was honed, out of necessity, during her time there. She claimed to have worked her way through by sweeping and scrubbing the school stairs. She later recollected "hard, barren years," which perhaps were these.[2] Her interest in the French language and culture likely began at Holy Names, where she studied both French and Spanish. The religious culture of the school also played an important role in Bonney's early life. On a list titled "Unforgettable People, Places, Things, Happenings" compiled many years later for her autobiography, Bonney included "R.C. [Roman Catholic] Experience" and "my godfather," a Catholic priest in California.[3] Years later, a friendship with Eugène Cardinal Tisserant of France

Paris storefronts by night were glittering illustrations of the role of lighting in modern design. OPPOSITE The Grand Bazar de l'Hôtel de Ville department store (55, rue de Verrerie) brilliantly illuminated as a parrot in a birdcage. ABOVE The massive glass and iron facade and cantilevered interior galleries of the Citröen automobile showroom (32, rue Marboeuf), designed by architects Albert Laprade and Léon-Emile Bazin, ca. 1929, enabled passersby to view all of the car models for sale in a single glance.

**Thérèse Bonney after being awarded
her Ph.D.** from the Sorbonne, 1921, age 27.
She was the youngest person, fourth woman,
and tenth American ever to achieve this honor.

led to her being granted exclusive permission to take photographs inside Vatican City—unprecedented access that resulted in her book *The Vatican*, published in 1939.

With aspirations to a career in teaching, she continued to study languages at the University of California, Berkeley, which she attended beginning in 1913. She graduated in 1916 with a bachelor of arts.[4] She earned money while at Berkeley by teaching French and Spanish at her high school. A significant step in her personal evolution was changing her second name from Teresa to the French equivalent Thérèse, which she did in 1916 while enrolled at Berkeley.[5] But she didn't turn her back on her native country. Although she never lived in California again after graduating from college, she proudly stated forty years later, "I'm as much a Californian as the poppy."[6]

In 1916 Bonney headed east to Cambridge, Massachusetts, to pursue a masters degree at Radcliffe College. She continued to support herself by teaching at a local school and giving private tutorials, but by the time she graduated in 1917, she had begun to think about a career outside of education. In a letter to her mother she confided, "One of the older teachers at Medford said to me this morning you ought not to be teaching—you're beyond it. You ought to take up something bigger."[7] Nevertheless, she spent the next two years at Columbia University in New York City, where she began her doctoral studies, an unusual achievement for a woman in the 1910s and early testament to Bonney's unflagging ambition.

By the summer of 1918 Bonney had become interested in theater and pursued it with characteristic passion. She took a job with the Théâtre du Vieux Colombier during their American season as private secretary to the company's director, Jacques Copeau. In the same year, she founded, with her sister Louise, what she claimed was the first bookshop in New York City devoted to French theater. She also became the official translator for Sarah Bernhardt's repertory, which was based in Paris.

Bonney made her first trip to Paris in 1919 when she was appointed by the American Association of Colleges to select students who would study in the United States as part of an exchange to foster relations among the allied nations during World War I.[8] By April of that year, she was working for the National Catholic War Council (NCWC) in Paris and preparing to complete her doctoral studies at the Sorbonne. In one of her earliest letters to her mother from the city that was to become her home for the next sixty years, Thérèse wrote, "Expect to like Paris—do already."[9]

The austere bookshop Edouard Loewy Librairie (137, boulevard Raspail), which Bonney described as "haunt of the modern bibliophile…designed in the modern mood by Claude Levy…paneling and furniture of oak combined with nickel tubing."

For the next three years Bonney worked for the NCWC and the Junior Red Cross, enjoyed a busy social life, and prepared her dissertation. Her post in the Junior Red Cross's Bureau of School Correspondence took her all over Europe and beyond as a lecturer.[10] These were good years. "I am getting much out of life," she wrote. "I almost cry

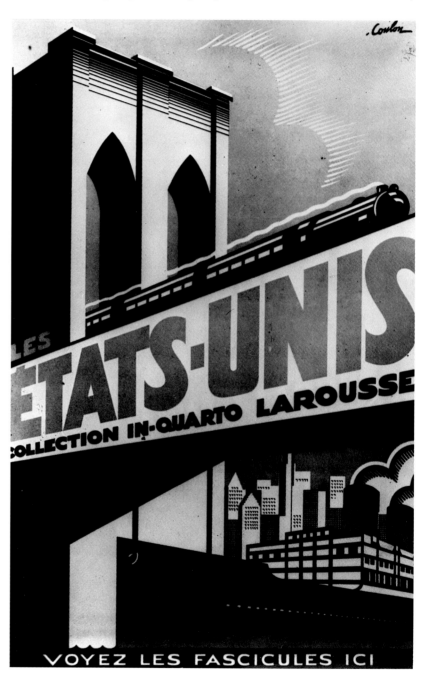

"Les Etats Unis" (United States) poster for the Larousse publishing house. With obvious patriotic interest in the subject, Bonney wrote, "America…interpreted by a modern poster artist Coulon for a famous publishing house, Larousse…. In the background, the skyline of New York, impressionistically stated…. An elevated train runs through the middle of the page…. With Coulon and others of the modern school of commercial art, typography plays an all important role."

as I write it—it has been so wonderful—so great…what a 'great, wide, wonderful world!'"[11] She also earned extra money during her student days "by translating the captions of the first American movies to be shown in Paris."[12] She attended the opera, theater, and lectures with American friends living in Paris. She also seems to have been embraced from the beginning by the intellectual community at the Sorbonne. She wrote in 1919: "One can have a dream of an evening dress for 65 or 70 dollars but as far as I can see nobody wears them, that is in intellectual circles and for the present those are mine."[13]

Bonney was awarded a Ph.D. from the Sorbonne in 1921.[14] She was the youngest individual, fourth woman, and tenth American to receive such an honor. "The moment is a great one," she recalled proudly.[15] Both the French and American press made quite a stir about her accomplishment, turning her into a minor celebrity. Bonney finally abandoned her plans to teach and instead went on to translate and adapt French plays for the American stage, and likewise, American plays for the French stage.[16] At the same time, the Bonney sisters founded their transcontinental business partnership, Thérèse in Paris and Louise in New York. In 1922, they were corresponding with American playwright Eugene O'Neill about obtaining the European rights to two of his works. In her sales pitch, Louise wrote: "We have just sold one play for production here, and sister is doing the translation of the Middleton plays to be presented there, and is to do two other important translations if things are accepted—one for the American stage, and one for the Odeon."[17] Thérèse also ventured into journalism in the first years of the 1920s as a columnist for the popular French newspaper *Le Figaro*. It was at this time that Bonney conceived the idea to take her own photographs to accompany her articles. And here this story begins.

_paris

In the aftermath of World War I Paris became a hub of creative expression—from fashion to fine arts to literature to design and beyond. The city's bohemian atmosphere attracted artists, writers, and intellectuals from all over the world. Tourists sought the Parisian experience they had read about in countless newspaper and magazine chronicles, especially in U.S. publications. Many American writers recorded Paris—its happenings, its personalities, and the city itself—in the 1920s and '30s. Among them

Delivery trucks represented a relatively new use of company logos as marketing tools. ABOVE The logo for furniture store Au Bûcheron (10, rue de Rivoli), by A.M. Cassandre, showed a woodcutter. OPPOSITE Monsavon's widely recognized logo, designed by the artist Jean Carlu, depicted the famous French stage and film star Maurice Chevalier. Carlu and Cassandre were highly regarded for their bold graphic designs.

was Janet Flanner, alias Genêt, who began writing her famous semimonthly "Letter from Paris" for *The New Yorker* in 1925. Bonney received a mention in Flanner's column in 1933 for her exhibition of daguerreotypes at the Galerie Pierre Colle in Paris. Society journals like *Town and Country* also featured regular columns on Paris. An entire body of literature documented the era, from Robert Forrest Wilson's 1924 *Paris on Parade*, to fictional accounts by F. Scott Fitzgerald and Ernest Hemingway.

Bonney's chronicle of Paris, by contrast, was primarily visual. In documenting modern design and architecture, she also recorded the vernacular of the city as well as its adoption of a modernist aesthetic—from avant-garde to more mainstream interpretations and hybrid expressions. She observed the city from the street, giving special attention to commercial art, storefronts, and window displays. She documented the rise

Bonney photographed modern graphic designs in isolation and in context. ABOVE Poster for Geugeot Automobiles, designed by Charles Loupot, 1926. Loupot blurred the image to convey speed and power—two important themes in Art Deco graphic design. RIGHT A parade of bold, modern posters typical of the era decorated a construction fence on the avenue des Champs-Elysées.

of advertising and graphic design as they were embraced by businesses. Modern advertising was the channel through which most of the public was informed not only of new products such as cosmetics and cars, but also of new art and design styles such as Art Deco. Bonney captured the work of several leading Parisian poster designers including Coulon, Charles Loupot, Jean Carlu, and A.M. Cassandre, and recorded the growing importance of logos as marketing tools. Her photos glorified not just what she called "the new school of commercial art," but the transformation of Paris itself in the modern era. For example, she captioned a photograph of a wall of temporary billboards around an old mansion being torn down on the avenue des Champs-Elysées: "The life of the past and its architecture give way to the constructions of new Paris."[18]

In addition to modern advertising methods, department store and boutique

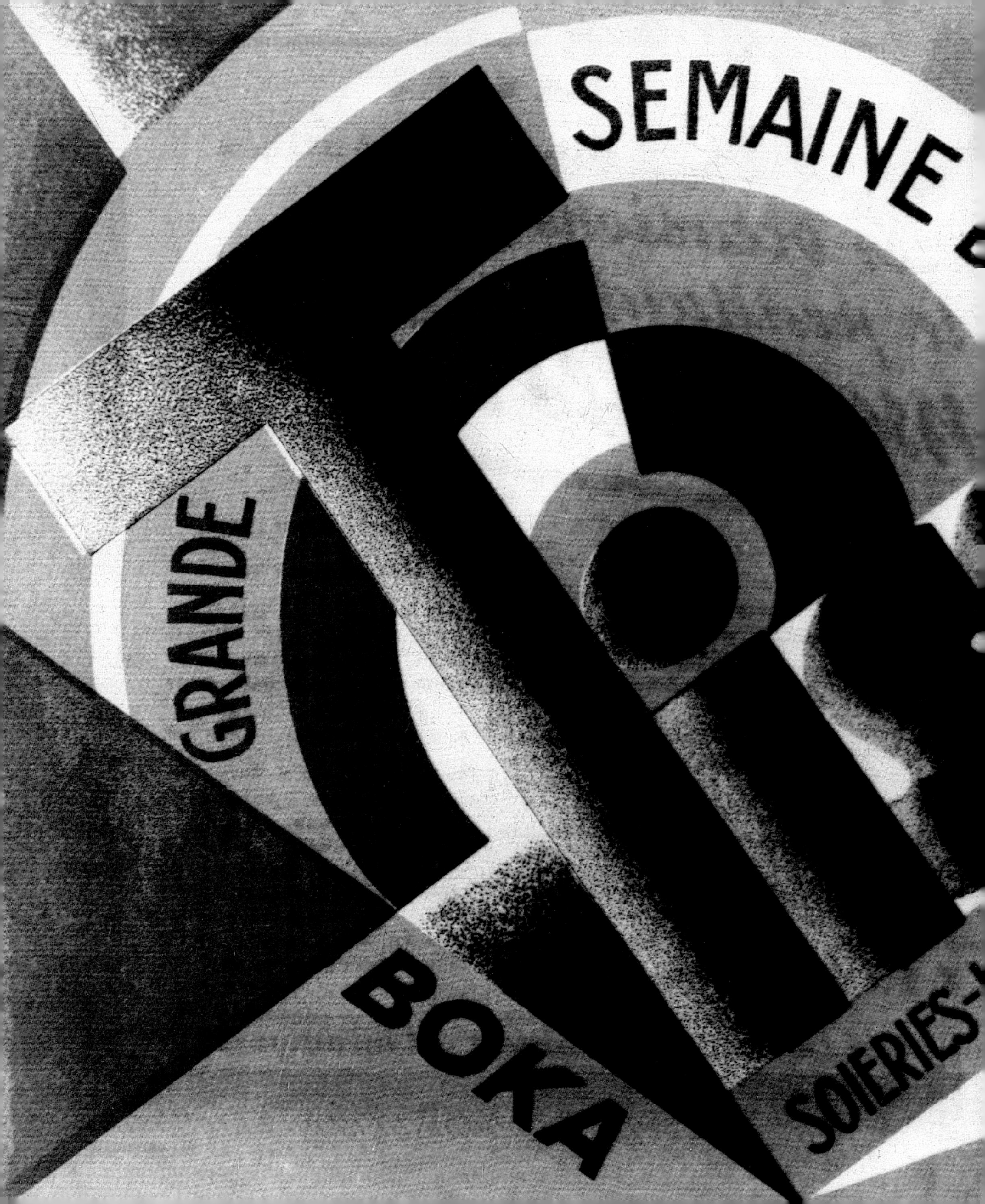
SEMAINE
GRANDE
BOKA
SOIERIES-

In this 1926 poster designed by Coulon
to promote a fabric sale, the background arcs were clearly
influenced by Eugène Chevreul's nineteenth-century theories
of simultaneous color contrast. Coulon's contemporaries
Robert and Sonia Delaunay also explored Chevreul's theories
in their works. The muscular typography and simple
graphics reflect the style of the 1920s.

A full range of Parisian storefronts was captured by Bonney's lens. TOP Dupont Barbier grocer's shop (3, rue Gomboust and 1, rue de Sontay), by Georges Djo-Bourgeois, ca. 1929. MIDDLE The opulent Art Deco facade of mannequin designer Pierre Imans' showroom (18, boulevard Haussmann), by Léon Leyritz. BOTTOM Roger et Gallet perfume shop (8, rue de la Paix), by architect Gauthier-Joseph Marrast. OPPOSITE Brodard & Taupin printer and bookbinder (4, rue Saint-Amand).

windows were crucial venues through which the public was advised of the newest products and trends, even if they merely passed by without entering the building. As window displays became more expressive, the culture of the *flâneur*, or stroller, was revived from its heyday in the late nineteenth century. Bonney followed closely the emergence of new boutiques in the city and the renovation of storefronts. These modern facades were frequently featured in French periodicals such as *Art et décoration* and in various American design and decorating magazines. They were also the subject matter for entire albums published in Paris in the 1920s and '30s. Avant-garde French architect René Herbst, creator of a number of shop interiors and window displays in Paris, proclaimed: "The street…is becoming a true democratic museum…that is constantly renewing itself…. Our modern architects demand that the public better comprehend what is being produced in their era."[19] In storefront photos, Bonney captured the full range of modern, from the austere to the luxurious, and its use from sales tool to genuine aesthetic experiment.

The progressive French architect Georges Djo-Bourgeois used strict geometry and almost no ornament in creating the facade for the grocer's shop Dupont Barbier. Its clean, bold, red letters were backlit against the white stucco surface of the building. Large expanses of glass in the front windows and door allowed a completely unobstructed view of the shop's interior. Another famous example was the clever and widely published facade of the book and record shop La Plaque Tournante, by French architect Pierre Barbe. In molded black staff or plaster, it emphasized the horizontal in its evocation of the grooves of a phonograph record. When illuminated in blue neon, the silver letters created an illusion that the facade was curved.[20] Much more ornate was that of the shop of Pierre Imans, a leading Parisian mannequin and display designer, on boulevard Haussmann. Mainly red and yellow marble, it contained illuminated columns of white opaque glass and lavish panels with images of Art Deco female mannequins. The polished metal of the sleek, modern lettering was repeated in the ornate pull-down shades that concealed the display window set back from the street.

By the 1920s, window display had evolved into a veritable art form, eulogized by architect L. P. (Louis-Pierre) Sézille as "a presentation in the form of an expressive symphony." Sézille believed that "more than expositions…[shrewd shopkeepers] contribute to the triumph of contemporary art by exposing the public at large to new forms."[21]

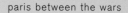

La Plaque Tournante book and record shop
(69, avenue Kléber), designed by architect Pierre Barbe,
ca. 1928. Created in black staff, a plaster-based building
material usually used for temporary structures, the facade
evoked the grooves of a phonograph record. By night,
when the silver lettering was lit in blue neon, La Plaque
Tournante appeared to be curved.

**Siégel was the leading mannequin and
display design firm** in Paris. Bonney considered
the Siégel boutique "one of the new sights of Paris by
night…strikingly modern store just opened on new French
boulevard has all the feeling modern decorative artists give
to new architecture with innovations in lighting effects."

Dramatic department store window display by Siégel. A bolt of dark fabric creates the dress's bodice and unexpected wings, while lighter fabric forms the fanned, tiered skirt and the display's background. This minimal and graphic window display was unusual for a traditional product like fabric, but stores hired Siégel for exactly this kind of bold gesture.

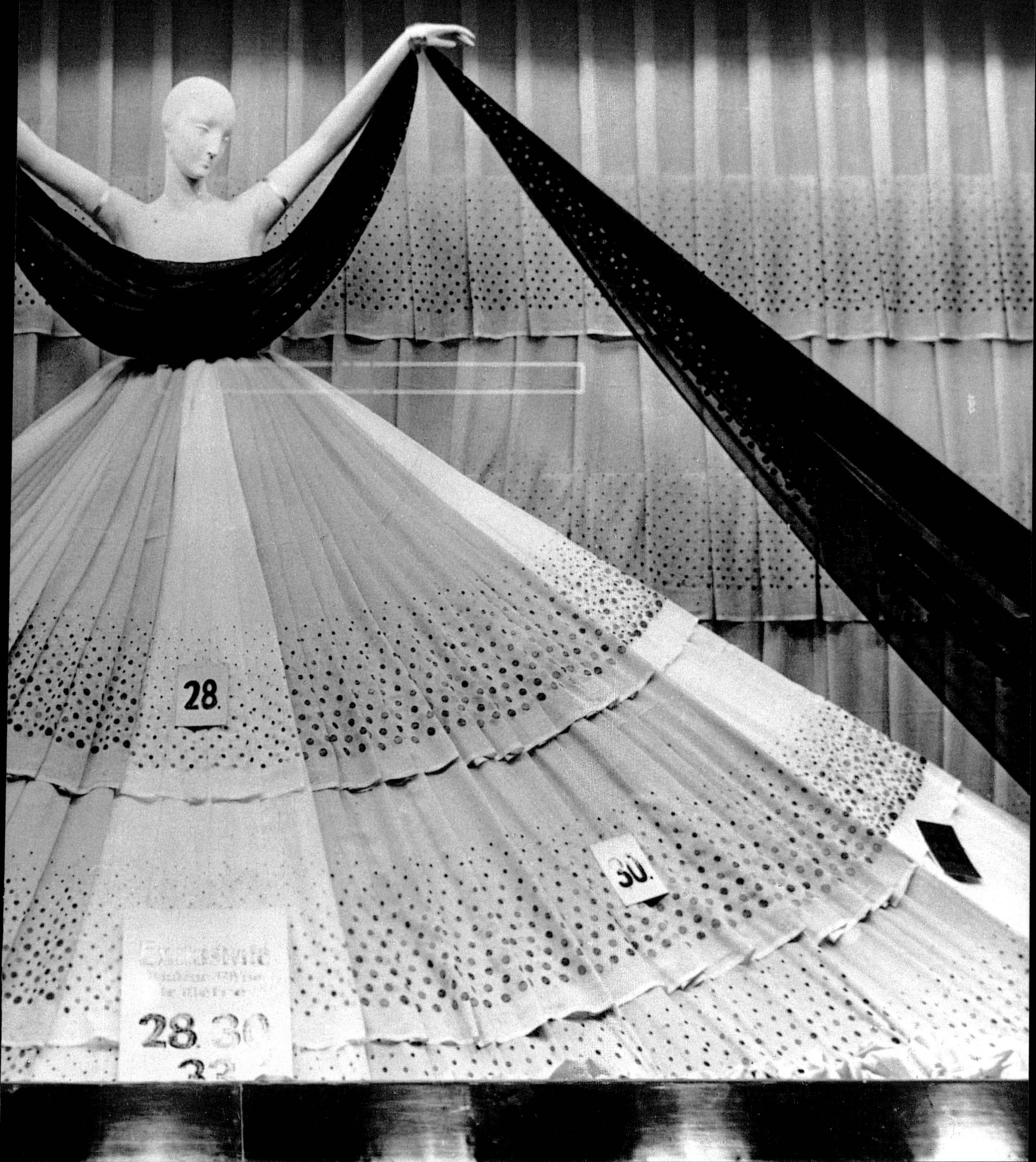
28.
30.
28. 30

Tennis clothing and equipment displayed
in abundance in the window of a Parisian department store.
Store windows were seen at the time as a sort of public
art gallery. Writers and designers believed that well-designed
storefronts and window displays could educate the public.
Passersby would absorb the latest aesthetics without
even having to enter the shop.

Women's shoes and stockings at Au Printemps department store (64, boulevard Haussmann), ca. 1929. Created by display designers Siégel, the theatrical array includes columns of stockings, dozens of shoes, and a bare female leg sprouting artful feathers. Large store windows for display and advertising were relatively new in the 1920s, and window display was an emerging art.

The annual Exposition de Blanc ("white sale," or sales on linens) spurred stores to create special facades and window displays. ABOVE Temporary exterior signage at Au Printemps department store featured Oriental motifs including a wooden pagoda and, in Bonney's words, "the sacred white elephants." OPPOSITE A whimsical display of children dancing in a garden of handkerchiefs advertised the sale at Maison de Blanc (6, boulevard des Capucines).

Some of the most compelling were created for the department stores, or *grands magasins*, including Au Printemps and Galeries Lafayette with their large windows and vast range of merchandise from which to draw inspiration. One effective approach was to group an abundance of one kind of merchandise—tennis rackets, dresses, or shoes— to completely fill the windows. "Feathers and finery of Paris, all the glamour associated with the French capital," is how Bonney described a lavish display of women's shoes and stockings at Au Printemps.[22] Complete with a female leg emerging from a bounty of flowing feathers, it was "daring, perhaps, but arresting."[23] Regular cut-price sales of bedlinens and towels—described by Bonney as "an event in the French family"—were responsible for consistently dynamic window displays, posters, catalogs, and special facades.[24] The Maison de Blanc, for example, once presented a wonderful fantasy garden made entirely of handkerchiefs. Children dressed in handkerchiefs frolicked around a glistening pool among trellises, trees, and grass.

Chiquito, Basque restaurant and bar (34, rue du
Colisée), by architect Charles Siclis. RIGHT The ground floor with
an illuminated glass fountain. OPPOSITE The spectacular
bi-level dining room. In *Where Paris Dines* (1929), Julian Street
noted: "Brightly lighted and decorated in ultra-modern style,
with a glass dance floor, through which coloured lights are
thrown, Chiquito is a comparatively new and quite popular
dancing restaurant with an atmosphere less formal than is
found at certain more extravagant establishments."

Thérèse Bonney's thorough documentation of the city also encompassed restaurants, cafés, bars, and theaters. She often photographed these establishments either before or after hours, but she also caught them at their most legendary moments: American artists gathered at Montparnasse's popular Café du Dôme, for example, and evenings at La Cigogne, The Jockey, and La Jungle nightclubs. Bonney also captured such haunts of the avant-garde as Le Grand Écart and Le Boeuf sur le Toit nightclubs, both made famous by the poet Jean Cocteau.[25] Hired to photograph jewelry by French couturier Lucien Lelong, she staged the shot at Le Grand Écart. The elegance of the jewelry, seen on a model's hand on the bar, deliberately matches the sophistication of the renowned nightclub.

The most popular nightclubs of Montmartre were part of Bonney's catalog. RIGHT Hired to photograph jewelry designed by Lucien LeLong, she staged the shot at Le Grand Écart (7, rue Fromentin). At the club—where, in the words of Julian Street, "young France [makes] whoopee…champagne not obligatory"—the jewelry became part of a larger narrative. OPPOSITE The facade of La Perruche (42, boulevard de Clichy) was painted several shades of green. At night, the signage and eyes of the massive wooden parakeet were illuminated in green.

The Jockey (146, boulevard du Montparnasse) was a
favorite with Man Ray and his companion, Kiki. Owned by the
American artist Hilaire Hiler and a former jockey named Miller,
the club was open from 1923 to 1930. Bonney often
photographed bars and clubs after hours, but here she
captured The Jockey with a crowd gathered in front.

Bonney photographed the patrons as well as the designs of legendary bars and nightclubs.
ABOVE The walls of La Cigogne ("the stork") nightclub (27, rue Bréa, Montparnasse) were decorated with a vibrant mural depicting an ensemble of storks playing jazz music.
OPPOSITE In the dining room in the new quarters of Le Boeuf sur le Toit (26, rue de Penthièvre), ca. 1928, the banquettes were upholstered in red leather, and parchment balloons and crystal orbs festooned the chandeliers (see also the bar on p.11).

Modern modes of transport—the ocean liner, the airplane—became important symbols of contemporary life in the interwar years, and as such were frequently translated into modern design. The architect Le Corbusier was particularly interested in the pure, functional design of ocean liners and the qualities of hygiene and order that design conveyed.[26] So too was Robert Mallet-Stevens: the inspiration of the ocean liner is particularly evident in his constructions on the rue Mallet-Stevens (discussed in further detail in chapter 4). The same theme was taken up by Charles Siclis in his striking interior for the Basque bar and nightclub Chiquito, designed to resemble a ship. This was, according to Bonney, the "latest rendez-vous of French capital… smart from aperitif hour thru to early hours of dawn."[27] A jazz band played on the

Théâtre Pigalle (12, rue Pigalle, Montmartre), by architect Charles Siclis, ca. 1929, at the request of Baron Henri de Rothschild. OPPOSITE The auditorium walls were sheathed in mahogany veneer because of the rare wood's exceptional acoustic properties. LEFT The extraordinary tubular steel grille in the lobby separated the public space from the dressing rooms of the actors. ABOVE Poster or program, designed by Jean Carlu, 1929.

second level, accessible on either side by a staircase. Chiquito's ground floor boasted an illuminated dance floor and a tubular fountain of opaque glass and polished metal, while curvilinear railings along the second level and the perimeter of the bar suggested the deck of a ship.

Just as dramatic as Chiquito was Charles Siclis's spectacular Théâtre Pigalle. Bonney's photo of the steel grille in the lobby is a beautifully abstract composition, while her photo of the main auditorium captures its many layers and spaces. She described Pigalle as "the most modern of Paris playhouses," and hoped the theater would promote "a new era in…drama."[28] Another modern venue was the Rody Bar, designed by French twin sculptors Joël and Jan Martel in 1928. The stark geometry of their design was carried through to the graphic elements. Squares and triangles are prominent in the typography, and the logo, seen on the building exterior and the front of the bar, uses a De Stijl–inspired motif. Cylinders form the interior and exterior lighting fixtures as well as a steep circular staircase behind the bar.

Travel and tourism were a perennial interest of Thérèse Bonney, pursued not only in the guidebooks she wrote with her sister, but in her role as pictorial consultant, for several years, to the Compagnie Générale Transatlantique. Ocean liners were the only means of transatlantic travel in the early twentieth century—by 1944, Bonney claimed

Rody Bar (76, rue Lafayette), designed by twin sculptors Joël and Jan Martel, 1928. The entire design scheme was created from geometric elements. OPPOSITE The staircase and lighting were cylindrical, and the De Stijl–inspired logo was echoed in the square tiles used on the wall and floor. A small Martel sculpture, similar to the concrete trees they created for Mallet-Stevens's garden at the 1925 Paris Exposition, was displayed behind the bar. LEFT Geometric elements were carried from the interior to the austere red and white facade and logo.

to have made the voyage more than one hundred times—and the 1920s and '30s saw the christening of a handful of new luxury French liners, including the *Île-de-France*, *L'Atlantique*, and *Normandie*. In 1927, Bonney photographed the interior of the *Île-de-France*, "the most luxurious ship afloat," shortly before its maiden voyage to New York that spring.[29] It boasted an unrivaled celebrity passenger list and a reputation as a floating party complete with an American jazz band. Bonney's agency undertook a full campaign to photograph the ship. Some of the resulting shots feature models lounging in cabins or salons; others show just interiors. Several Art Deco designers, including Jacques-Emile Ruhlmann, René Prou, Atelier Martine, Jean Dunand, Etienne

The Île-de-France ocean liner, launched in 1927, was the collaborative creation of a team of Art Deco designers and architects, led by Pierre Patout. OPPOSITE The opulent grand salon. LEFT The lighting of the marble staircase to the first-class dining room was designed by René Lalique. The columns on either side were over 26 feet high. ABOVE This stateroom, designed by René Prou, was first exhibited by the Compagnie Générale Transatlantique in the French Pavilion at the 1925 Paris Exposition.

Paris's modern hotels were often designed by leading architects and interior designers. The lounge and entrance of the Hôtel de Paris (8, boulevard de la Madeleine) were designed by architects Emile Molinie and Charles Nicod and decorated by Société Noël with glasswork by René Lalique and ironwork by Edgar Brandt.

In the Hôtel de Londres et Milan (8, rue Saint-Hyacinthe), designed by Etienne Kohlmann, the dining room was decorated with dark red murals that stood out against the neutral walls and white tablecloths. Hotels became palaces of design in this period, as new modes of transportation made travel easier and more appealing.

Couturière and milliner Suzanne Talbot,
ca. 1929. Of Talbot, Bonney playfully warned, "Be Careful!
You may emerge looking very smart and perhaps a trifle
wicked, for what Suzanne cannot do with a few yards
of material in a turban, or the normal outlines of a brim,
or that tiny little vail [*sic*], isn't worth conceiving!"

Kohlmann, René Lalique, and Henri Navarre, collaborated on the ship's interior scheme under the direction of chief architect Pierre Patout of France, who also designed the interiors of *L'Atlantique* and *Normandie*. Remarkably, each of the 450 first-class and luxury cabins was unique. The overall style combined elements of modernism with more classicizing treatments. The staircase and flanking columns that led to the first-class dining room, for example, were constructed of Pyranese marble with nickel banisters and lighting by Lalique. A massive historic map of the Île-de-France province covered the wall behind. Individual beds replaced berths in the staterooms. Prou's elegant cabin featured angular rosewood beds carved with flowers and covered in plush velvet spreads. Back on land, Bonney also documented the interiors of some of the notable new hotels in and around the city, including the Hôtel de Paris with interior schemes by Ruhlmann, Société Noël, Edgar Brandt, and Lalique; the Hôtel Londres et Milan designed by Kohlmann; and the Grand Hôtel in Tours designed by Pierre Chareau.

Another glimpse of the city and the era is granted by Bonney's portraits of its inhabitants. She photographed hundreds of artists, writers, musicians, designers, couturiers, architects, scientists, feminists, and the elite, from painters Henri Matisse, Georges Braque, and Marie Laurencin to expatriates Edith Wharton, George Antheil, and Nancy Cunard. These images were extensively published in the *New York Times* during these decades. Her portraits of the elegant couturière Suzanne Talbot (Madame Mathieu Lévy) and the whimsical artist Alexander Calder were particularly successful in capturing the spirit of their subjects.

_the bonney photographs

"From 1922," Bonney wrote, "…I built up a photographic documentation of the modern decorative and design movement in France…recording all the Salon manifestations, private commissions executed by different architects, decorators and designers. I still have a very significant and representative collection.…They ought to be in the archives of some institution like yours."[30]

The late 1930s marked the eve of World War II and Bonney's intended move from Paris back to New York. They also marked the end of an era for her in this genre of photography. Between 1937 and 1940, Bonney relinquished her incomparable collection to the Cooper Union Museum for the Arts of Decoration as both a sale and gift. The museum had been established in 1897 as a rich and outstanding archive of international examples from which professional designers and design students could draw inspiration.[31] Bonney's photographs were an invaluable addition.

These photographs tell the story of a unique and exciting moment in history. They record modern French design and life, but also the adoption of modern in America. Of course this collection is in no way a complete narrative of the era or of modernism; it represents the particular experience of its author. It is what Bonney saw in Paris between the wars. With her Graflex camera, she captured the work not only of such leaders of the modern movement as architect Pierre Chareau and silversmith Jean Puiforcat, but also of figures less known today, including designers Renée Kinsbourg and American-born Lucie Holt Le Son (pp.126–27), two of a number of women whose work was recognized by Bonney. While examples of some if not many of the furniture and decorative objects she photographed exist today, most of the private and public interiors, as well as the storefronts, do not. Her eye for detail, through which she captured numerous unexpected elements, adds a boon to decorative arts connoisseurs. Just as important as the photographs themselves are Bonney's captions. Descriptive, engaging, and sometimes witty, they almost always draw attention to what is modern about the image. The anecdotes they often provide enhance our understanding of the subject and the era. Bonney's recognition of the historic importance of her collection, and her decision to entrust it to a public museum rather than a private collector, have ensured that her vision has continued to educate, inform, and inspire.

American artist Alexander Calder at work in his studio in Paris, where he lived off and on between 1926 and 1933. Bonney photographed some of the most notable personalities of the Parisian fashion, art, and design communities between the wars.

2_an american in paris

Thérèse Bonney founded the Bonney Service—the first American illustrated press service in Europe—around 1923.[1] Headquartered in her Paris studio, it also boasted a satellite office in New York in the Bonney family apartment. Frustrated with experiencing life only through books, she wanted to gain "real contacts with the raw material of life, with the men and women who made up the colorful stimulating pageant of Modern European life."[2] Although there were varying accounts published in the press at the time regarding where, when, and why she started taking photographs herself, most agree that she took her earliest photos to illustrate her own articles and that she soon hired other photographers to objectify her vision.[3] Bonney never documented any formal photography training of her own and was very likely self-taught. Unlike many other female photographers of her era working in Europe—including Lucia Moholy, Florence Henri, and Berenice Abbott—Bonney valued purely documentary work and commercial success over photographic experimentation or artistic expression.[4] In fact, in an interview many years later, she admitted to having never "been interested in the camera as a piece of apparatus" or having even a full understanding of its "technology."[5] Nonetheless—or even perhaps because of this—her focus on running a photographic agency and her interest in modern design led to a unique and compelling collection of photographs of Paris between the wars.

Fashion and beauty were of perennial interest to Bonney, and in the 1920s Paris was perhaps the consummate place to delight in them. OPPOSITE Model wearing a bracelet designed by the fashion house Worth and carrying a dog's-head walking stick by Hermès. Bonney observed that "the latest whim of the Parisienne is to have her own dog's-head on her cane...made in unbreakable plaster by her favorite artist." ABOVE A fashionable coiffure.

In the mid-1920s, Bonney's studio-office was located at 82, rue des Petits Champs, designed and decorated in a modern style by the avant-garde Turkish architect Gabriel Guévrékian. Trained in Vienna, Guévrékian collaborated on a number of projects with architect Robert Mallet-Stevens, including the construction of the rue Mallet-Stevens. By 1930, Bonney had moved just down the street to 76, rue des Petits Champs, to an apartment that she had decorated by French architect Louis Sognot (pp. 168–69). Throughout the 1920s, Sognot directed the design atelier of Au Printemps department

Thérèse and Louise Bonney shared apartments in Paris and New York. In their book *A Shopping Guide to Paris*, the sisters invited readers to visit: "We keep open house at our Paris address and shall be glad to help you." ABOVE Terrace and glass-enclosed bar of the Bonney apartment in Paris (82, rue des Petits Champs), designed by Gabriel Guévrékian, ca. 1927. In front of a banner of Stehli Silks' "Manhattan" print by Clayton Knight are two Pierre Chareau chairs covered in a black-and-white pony-print textile. RIGHT Louise Bonney, ca. 1930.

store, Primavera, and created several functionalist interiors in collaboration with the French designer Charlotte Alix.

Bonney employed three photographers and six secretaries and had two photographic laboratories. She supplied photographs to newspapers, magazines, and illustrated books in several countries as well as to some of the largest syndicates including the Associated Press and Wide World. She claimed, in 1931, to distribute an average of 350 photographs a month worldwide, 200 of which were published in the United States.[6] In Europe, her work was frequently published in France and Germany, among other countries.[7] It also appeared with some regularity in England.

Thérèse ran the Bonney Service in partnership with her sister Louise and their mother Addie; Louise oversaw the daily operation of the Manhattan office in addition to her own journalistic endeavors, and Addie managed the U.S. sales of the Bonney photographs.[8] Louise became an accomplished critic of art and design in New York during the 1920s and '30s, publishing articles on modern design in such periodicals as *Good Furniture and Decoration, Atelier, Arts & Decoration,* and *House & Garden*—though, because her writings nearly always focused on American design, they were not accompanied by Thérèse's photographs. She also acted as a public relations consultant and was hired by the American textile designer Ruth Reeves in 1928 to promote her involvement with a line of textiles designed for Macy's department store.[9] Louise's most influential roles in the field were her positions on the Board of Design and as Director of the "America at Home" exhibit of the 1939–40 New York World's Fair.[10] Although Thérèse visited New York twice a year to meet with newspaper and magazine editors, Louise was responsible to a certain degree for the promulgation of the Bonney Service photographs in America.[11] Addie Bonney oversaw much of the negotiation with the Cooper Union Museum for the sale of the Bonney Service prints in 1937. She also went on to place her daughter's wartime photographs in American publications, and remained Thérèse's New York representative until her own death in 1945.[12]

_fashion

Bonney's service initially focused on fashion and expanded to "interiors, exteriors, everything from pure art to gadgets."[13] Thérèse Bonney was part of an emerging contingency of female photographers in Europe in the 1920s, including Madame D'Ora

In her fashion photography Bonney documented both clothing and accessories. This model is wearing jewelry by Gérard Sandoz—including rings, bracelets, pendant, and hat pin of lacquer, emeralds, rubies, and other brilliants— and a dinner ensemble by Suzanne Talbot, including gold straw turban with blue net veil, and a blue coat over a white silk dress, ca. 1928.

Beach ensemble including swimsuit, robe, umbrella, and blanket designed by Mary Nowitsky. "Are you ready for the real Lido, or the American Lido—Palm Beach," asked Bonney. "For there is as much competition on these beaches now as there used to be in a drawing room of the nineties, and your 'place in the social sun' may be gained or lost here. Mary Nowitsky is the one creator in Paris who will do all this for you, so that you will appear in a blaze of glory."

Designer luxury goods were often packaged in equally luxurious containers. FAR LEFT ABOVE Pendant designed by A.M. Cassandre for jeweler Georges Fouquet, ca. 1925. FAR LEFT BELOW Bracelets by Gérard Sandoz. MIDDLE ABOVE Louis Vuitton "Heures d'Absence" perfume in etched crystal bottle and gold box. MIDDLE BELOW Schiaparelli Undertone skin product in Art Deco bottle and slipcase box. (This photo may not have been shot by Bonney, since the back of the Cooper-Hewitt print is stamped "M. Pettinati, London.") NEAR LEFT Limited edition perfume bottles designed by Sèvres for couturière Jeanne Lanvin. BELOW Woman's bracelet and ring and man's ring, designed by Gérard Sandoz.

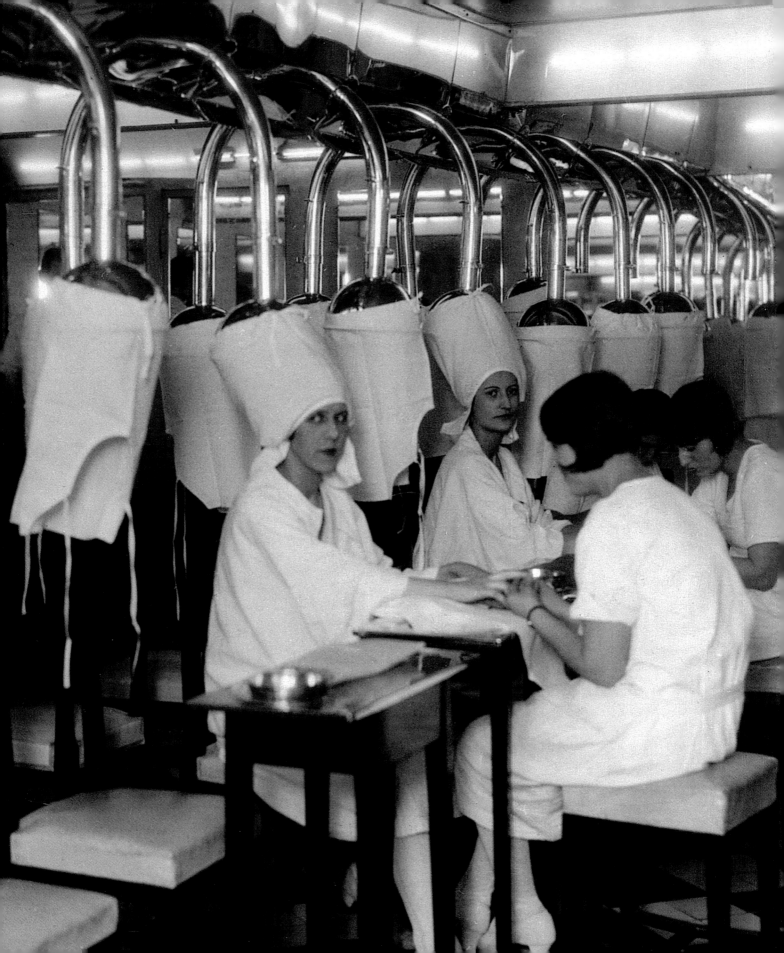

and Germaine Krull, who were breaking into the traditionally male realm of fashion photography.[14] Bonney's fashion photographs appeared regularly in such newspapers as the *New York Sun*, the *New York Herald Tribune*, and the *New York Times* between approximately 1925 and 1935. From 1923 through 1928, Bonney was Paris Fashion Editor of the *New York Times*, Feature and Paris Fashion Editor of the *Mid-Week Pictorial*, and Special Representative of Wide World Photos (the last two were

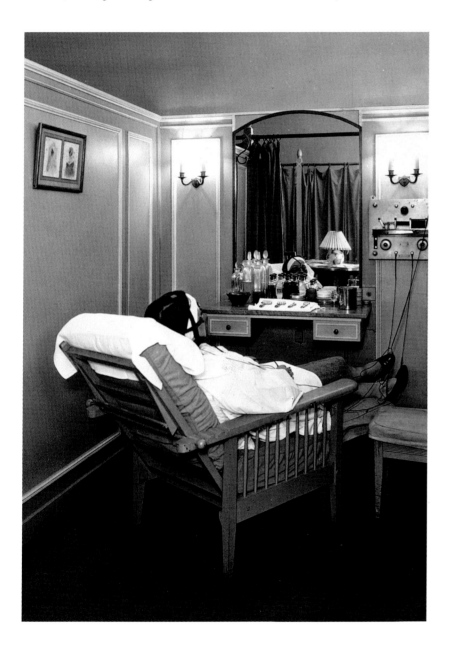

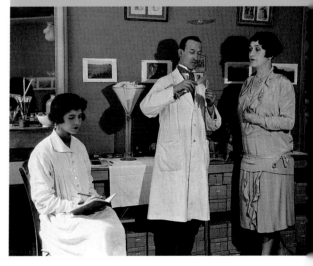

Paris's fashionable salons are the subject of some of Bonney's most amusing photos. OPPOSITE Clients in the hair and manicure room at the Antoine salon (5, rue Cambon). Bonney aptly described them as "A roomful of strange-looking creatures." LEFT Private treatment room at the Lina Cavalieri beauty salon (61, avenue Victor-Emmanuel-III). The somewhat alarming electrical apparatus strapped to the client's head is part of a facial treatment. ABOVE Laboratory experiment at the Lina Cavalieri salon. Cavalieri is pictured at far right.

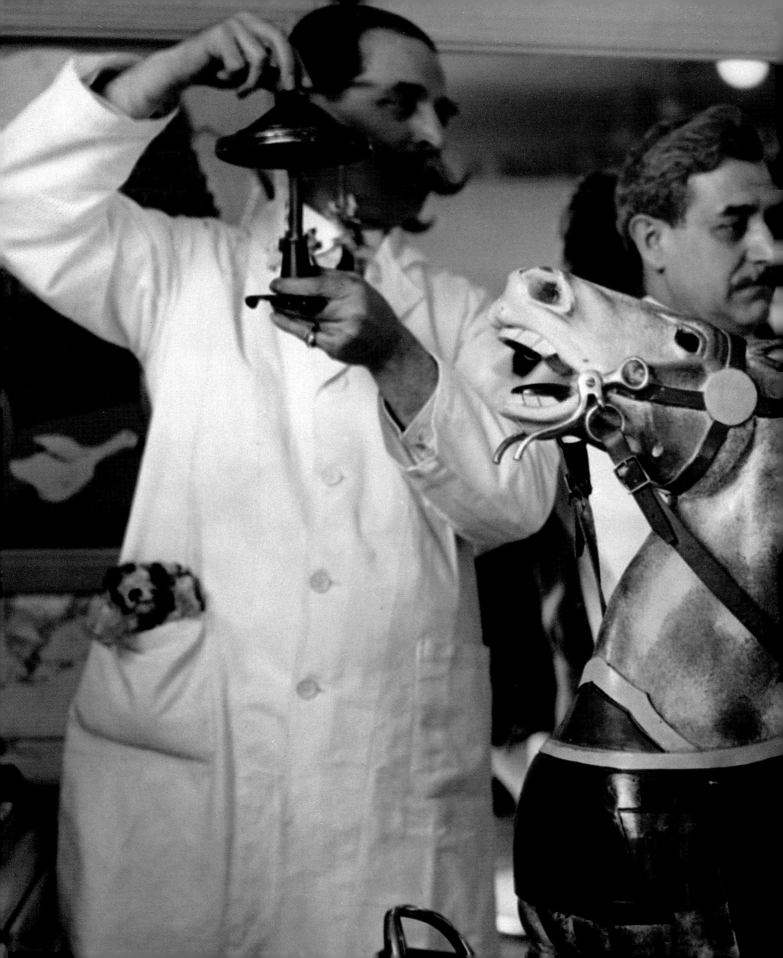

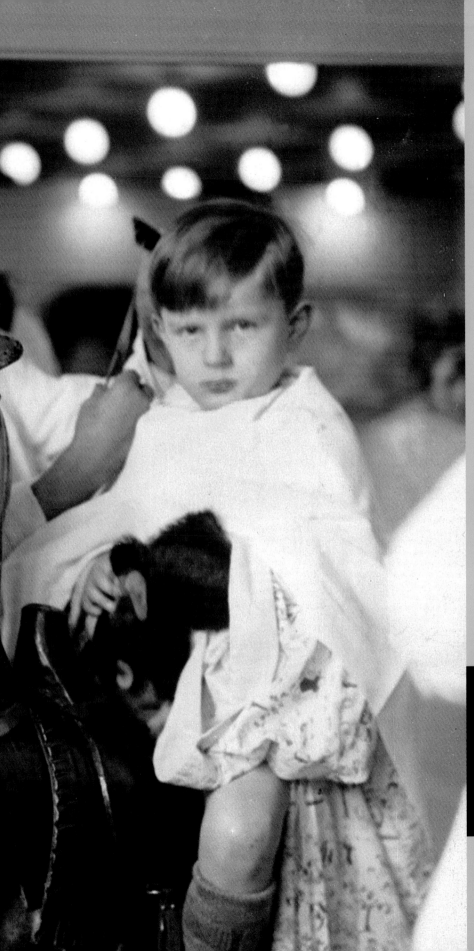

The children's barber shop at Au Printemps department store (64, boulevard Haussmann) was filled with distractions. The barbers were, in the words of Bonney, "ready for action…not for warfare, but for haircutting… modern barber's shop for children at Printemps offers adjustable rocking horses to replace the classic chairs for its small but important clientele."

subsidiaries of the *New York Times*.)[15] Her fashion work documented accessories as well as entire collections from Parisian designers such as Italian-born Elsa Schiaparelli.[16] Although her fashion photographs never appeared on the editorial pages of the most prestigious fashion magazines, they were used in advertisements in *Vogue* and *Harper's Bazaar*.

Within the realm of fashion and beauty, Bonney was also involved with advertising campaigns for Palmolive soap—at the time a fine facial soap—which brought her into some of the most fashionable salons of Paris: Coiffeur Vincent and beauty specialist Madame Payout both promoted the famous product. She went on to photograph the elegant salons of Lina Cavalieri and Antoine, among others, documenting new techniques and the salon spaces themselves. "Antoine in Paris is an experience!" she wrote. "The world and its neighbor gather there and truly rub elbows in the crowded shampoo room. You will never dare throw any stones after having lived an hour in this glass house."[17] (Bonney also photographed the flamboyant coiffeur's famous glass house on rue Saint-Didier, pp.118–19.) Although a staunch modernist, Bonney

Many hairdressers ("coiffeurs") and beauty specialists in Paris, including Vincent, Antoine, and Helena Rubenstein, were recognized as minor celebrities as early as the 1910s and '20s. ABOVE The coiffeur Vincent with a client in his salon (20, rue Royale), in a Palmolive soap advertisement. RIGHT Entrance of the Helena Rubenstein salon (52, rue du Faubourg Saint-Honoré), designed by Atelier Martine, with silver and purple ceilings and walls and sheer silver curtains.

found that Helena Rubenstein's sleek Paris salon "hasn't quite the charm of her really stunning New York house," which was more ornate.[18] Designed by couturier Paul Poiret's design firm Atelier Martine, the typically bold Art Deco color scheme of Rubenstein's spartan reception area was silver and "Poiret purple."[19]

As the co-author of *A Shopping Guide to Paris*, Thérèse Bonney was evidently personally interested in the city's luxury goods. She photographed the interiors and merchandise of some of the most beautiful boutiques in the French capital. These included several perfume shops, among them the elegant Roget et Gallet store, and Richard Hudnut's decadent, Art Deco shop designed by French architect Jacques Debat-Ponsan. The latter was richly ornamented with exotic palm trees and geometricized flowers. Scalloped edges were repeated on the glass chandelier, tables, chair backs, and moldings. The liberal use of glass created a highly reflective environment. Illustrator Georges Barbier created a fantastical mural set in a mirrored niche at the back of the salon. The club chairs were covered in Charles Martin's "Ananas" (pineapples) woven silk for Bianchini Férier.

Parisian shoe boutiques also fascinated Bonney, who photographed several in the 1920s and '30s. Shoe designer André Perugia, she wrote, "knows the value of publicity,

Richard Hudnut perfume shop (18–20, rue de la Paix), designed by architect Jacques Debat-Ponsan (above). The illustrator Georges Barbier designed some of the interior elements of this thoroughly Art Deco salon, including a fantastical mural set in a mirrored niche at the back of the shop. Hudnut also had an elegant, modern salon on Fifth Avenue in New York City designed by architects Ely Jacques Kahn and Eliel Saarinen.

Parisian shoe boutiques competed for the attentions of style-conscious shoppers. OPPOSITE Perugia (11, rue du Faubourg Saint-Honoré), ca. 1927. LEFT Display at the Julienne boutique (235, rue Saint-Honoré). Julienne designed shoes for the couturier Worth. ABOVE TOP Enzel (6, rue du Faubourg Saint-Honoré), designed by architect Raymond Nicolas, ca. 1929. ABOVE Nickeled copper footrest, smoking stand, and floor mirror designed by Francis Jourdain for the Bally shoe boutiques (11, boulevard de la Madeleine and 35, boulevard des Capucines), designed by Robert Mallet-Stevens, ca. 1928.

The interiors of Parisian department stores
were as interesting to Bonney as their window displays. ABOVE
Glove counter at the upscale Robert Bély department store
(45, rue des Mathurins), designed by Pierre Patout. Bonney
considered this "the first deluxe department store in the French
capital, and the largest ultra-modern shop built by the famous
architect of modern stores Pierre Patout." RIGHT Crisscrossing
stairs bisect the main floor of Robert Bély. OPPOSITE Women
ride the newly installed escalators in Au Printemps.

The main floor of Au Printemps department store after the original open rotunda was floored over to create additional space. The new pink ceiling was illuminated by three tiers of lights lining its perimeter. Jewelry and perfume were displayed in the cabinets below.

having proved it still more by planning and executing the first modern shoe shop in Paris. It was the talk of the city for some time with its snake skin doors and furniture. These dramatic ideas marked him, and the smart world followed…."[20] Designed in 1927, the Perugia showroom (p.80) featured black and yellow marble columns and angular black lacquer chairs covered in boa skin and upholstered in green velvet.[21] The walls were concrete and polished granite. Curtains of Rodier fabric gave added privacy to this exclusive and expensive boutique, a favorite among the rich and famous.

Architect Raymond Nicolas created the strikingly modern shop for Enzel, another popular women's shoe boutique, located on the rue du Faubourg Saint-Honoré (p.81). Concrete walls and hard aluminum moldings achieved a thoroughly modern aesthetic. All the fittings and fixtures were marble. The lively, abstract designs of the display window and door, executed in glass and aluminum, gave the store a dynamic atmosphere.

In addition to the smart boutiques of Paris, Bonney also captured the interiors of the city's spectacular department stores. She noted the modernization of Au Printemps when it installed its first set of elevators and inserted a floor in its great rotunda to create additional retail space. Architect Pierre Patout, who typically favored the sumptuous, designed what she proclaimed to be "Paris' first deluxe department store": Robert Bély, on rue des Mathurins (p.82). Its dramatic iron staircase by Raymond Subes extended from the basement to the top floor. All fittings and woodwork were ebonized, the walls concrete, and the floor a robust geometric pattern in blue and gray rubber. The forms of the lighting reflected the angular elements found throughout.[22]

The fashion world provided Thérèse Bonney with more than modern imagery; it gave her the material for her largest written work. Although marketed as a travel companion, Bonney's book *A Shopping Guide to Paris* was actually an exhaustive discussion of the fashion scene in Paris including dressmakers, couturiers, and boutiques, where to find them, and in some cases, specific employees to speak with once you arrived. She also dedicated chapters to shopping for children and men, antiques and modern design, restaurants, beauty salons, and even medical practitioners should an emergency arise. Today, *A Shopping Guide to Paris* is standard reference material for fashion and design historians of interwar Paris.

Dressing room for an artist created for the annual Exposition de la Décoration Contemporaine, 1930. The installation was designed by André Lavezzari for Soubrier, and the dressing gown was by Jeanne Lanvin, whom Bonney considered a couturière "of the highest rank."

In fashion's capital, couture salons were newsworthy, and Bonney captured a full range, from those of legendary figures like Madeleine Vionnet and Paul Poiret to the lesser-known Marie Bordes and Madame Lipska. ABOVE Curved staircase at Marie Bordes's salon (rue Saint-Honoré), designed by architect Pierre Barbe and decorated by Madame Myrbor. RIGHT Fitting room in the salon of Madame Lipska (146, avenue Champs-Elysées), designed by Lipska herself with a burnished copper screen and natural tulip-wood walls streaked in pink.

Fashion designer Madeleine Vionnet
in 1926, working with the wooden mannequin on which
she always designed. Vionnet's innovations included the
bias cut, which created a close, flattering, and feminine
fit. Bonney found Vionnet's designs to embody "a very
practical, ageless beauty, for a Vionnet gown is the same
yesterday, to-day, and to-morrow." Her friendship with
Vionnet was one of her closest and longest lasting.

_friends

While working in fashion, Bonney forged several important friendships with, among
others, Madeleine Vionnet, Elsa Schiaparelli, and Sonia Delaunay. Her friendship with
Vionnet was one of her closest and longest, lasting from 1921 until the dressmaker's
death in 1975.[23] Delaunay and Schiaparelli very likely introduced Bonney to the communities of avant-garde artists to which both designers belonged. These friendships,
however, were not limited to mutual interests in fashion and art; both lasted at least
through World War II and survived the hardships faced by artists during those years. In
the 1920s, Bonney photographed Elsa Schiaparelli, her collections, and her salon in
Paris. In her autobiography *Shocking Life*, the legendary fashion designer wrote, "I have
been privileged to be associated with some extraordinary women. In the realm of
warfare I happened to work side by side with them, and most of them have been Americans—Anne Morgan, her publicity agent Gilliam, Isabelle Kemp, Kathleen Hales,
Thérèse Bonney, and Florence Conrad."[24] Sonia Delaunay, wife of Cubist painter
Robert Delaunay, was a highly regarded painter who began designing textiles and
clothing in the 1920s. Bonney bought Sonia Delaunay's fashions as early as 1924,
modeled and photographed her clothing, and photographed Delaunay herself. In his
biography of Sonia Delaunay, Axel Madsen writes about a chance meeting between
the Delaunays and Bonney in the summer of 1941 in Nîmes. "Their American friend
was on her way home, with exit visas and railway tickets to Lisbon. 'Not that I'm across
the ocean yet,' she smiled. 'Visas don't protect anyone from mines.' The three of them
convinced the surly hotel manager to serve a small meal in the Delaunays' room. Robert
sat up in bed as they talked about the dresses Sonia had made and Theresa [Thérèse]
photographed, and the old days at the Closerie des Lilas and the Dôme, the impassioned
arguments over abstract art. They'd see each other soon, they agreed as Theresa left.
Peace could not be far away. Five days later, Germany invaded the Soviet Union."[25]

Other friends in Paris in the 1920s and '30s included the artist Raoul Dufy, who
painted Bonney's portrait three times, and whose work she tirelessly promoted both
before and after his death in 1953. She even arranged medical treatments for him in the
United States that prolonged his life. Bonney also counted among her friends the artists
Georges Rouault, who painted her portrait six times, and Alice Halicka, who painted
both Thérèse and her apartment. She certainly knew and may also have been personal

friends with a number of renowned designers, including Jean Lurçat; architect Pierre Chareau, whose work was heavily represented in her private collection;[26] and Robert Mallet-Stevens, one of the most important and avant-garde French architects between the two world wars. Mallet-Stevens was influenced early on by the work of Viennese Secession architect (and founder of the Wiener Werkstätte) Josef Hoffmann, who favored geometric forms in an obvious rejection of the Art Nouveau style. During his prolific career, Mallet-Stevens designed a number of private residences, including the Villa de Noailles (pp.113–15), his first built work, and the rue Mallet-Stevens, the Paris street on which he designed each of the atelier-houses, including his own (pp.176–78). Other projects included commercial buildings such as the Alfa-Romeo Garage and the Bally shoe stores; world's fairs including those held in Paris in 1925 and 1937 (pp.136–47); salon installations; and the design of furniture. He frequently collaborated with a number of progressive fellow designers including Francis Jourdain, Jean Prouvé, sculptors Joël and Jan Martel, and glass designer Louis Barillet.[27] Thérèse Bonney documented Mallet-Stevens's work extensively. In an introduction she contributed to a 1930 monograph, she conveyed both personal and professional respect for him: "As a man and as artist he expresses the best of his time."[28]

Thérèse Bonney's American friends in Paris included writers Janet Flanner and Gertrude Stein; textile designer Ruth Reeves; and Katherine Dreier, founder with Marcel Duchamp of the Société Anonyme.[29] She did not, however, belong to the famous group of American literary expatriates centered around Sylvia Beach's Left Bank bookshop Shakespeare & Co. In fact several years later she dismissively recalled, "Hemingway and Fitzgerald? Sure I knew them, but they didn't belong to my world. I lived in a world where people earned their living."[30]

_beyond photography

In addition to her press service, Bonney took on a number of commissions to promote American design in Europe. This included a line of "Americana" dress silks by Stehli Silks Corporation designed by some of the United States's most notable artists, including photographer Edward Steichen, and depicting jazz bands, roller coasters, and the like (pp.92–94). Steichen's designs, adapted from his photographs of everyday objects such as mothballs, sugar cubes, and carpet tacks, were the most abstract in the collection.

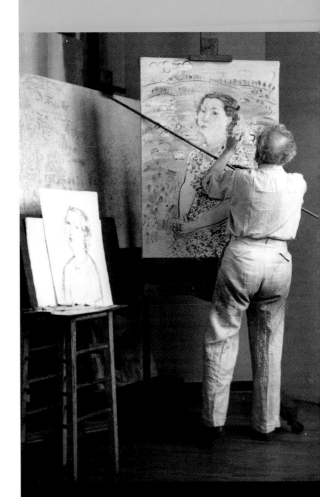

Raoul Dufy painting a portrait of Thérèse Bonney, ca. 1938. Dufy was another of Bonney's most intimate friends. He painted her portrait three times, and her private art collection boasted a number of his works. Bonney promoted Dufy's work throughout her career by organizing exhibitions of his paintings and even attempting to produce a film on his life and work, though this was ultimately never made.

Sonia Delaunay, painter and designer of textiles, fashion, and furniture, photographed in the 1930s. Thérèse Bonney was both a friend and client of the versatile Delaunay as early as 1924. Bonney even modeled Delaunay's clothing (sold through her boutique at 19, boulevard Malesherbes), which was particularly popular among the Parisian avant-garde.

Prints from the "Americana" collection
of Stehli Silks Corporation, New York, in silk crêpe de
chine. RIGHT "Thrill," by Dwight Taylor, ca. 1926. With a
strong machine-age aesthetic in dark blue on a white
ground, "Thrill" captured a distinctly American form
of popular entertainment—the roller coaster. OPPOSITE
"Rhapsody," by John Held Jr., ca. 1926, depicted American
jazz, which was all the rage in 1920s Paris.

Bonney also organized a number of exhibitions between the wars in both Paris and New York, all of which were widely covered in the American press. The first, a series of photographs from Bonney's private collection entitled "L'Epoque 1900/Gay 90s," was shown in Paris at Galeries Georges Petit in 1932. It then traveled to the Knoedler Gallery in New York and other institutions including the Newark Museum and the Milwaukee Art Institute. These photographs inspired her book *Remember When? A Pictorial Chronicle of the Turn of the Century and of the Days Known as Edwardian*, published in 1933 with a foreword by Gibson Girls creator, illustrator Charles Dana Gibson. Another exhibition, "The Second Empire by Louis-Jacques Daguerre and His School," a selection of rare daguerreotypes also from her private collection, opened at Galerie Pierre Colle in Paris in 1933. It too went to the Knoedler Gallery and then to the National Gallery in Washington, D.C. In the mid-1930s, Bonney served as the director of the Gallery for French Art in La Maison Française, at New York's Rockefeller Center. She organized four shows for the gallery, the first of which was the "Lafayette Centenary Exhibition" in 1934, which was planned in cooperation with a show at the Louvre on the anniversary of the famous revolutionary aristocrat's death. This was followed by "Famous Women of French History," "Normandy: the Province, its People and the Ship," and "Napoleon," all in 1935. Gallery board member and friend Anne Morgan praised Bonney as having a "rare understanding of Franco-American relations."[31] It was precisely because of this and also her efforts in promoting French art in the United States that she was awarded the Chevalier de la Légion d'Honneur in 1934.

"Carpet Tacks," designed by Edward Steichen,
1927, from the "Americana" prints range of Stehli Silks
Corporation, in silk crêpe de chine. This print was one of
several in the collection that were created from Steichen's
photographs of such everyday objects as moth balls,
sugarcubes, buttons, and thread.

_celebrity

In 1924 the American journalist and art critic Helen Appleton Read described Thérèse Bonney as an "international." Read defined such internationals as the foreigners, mainly Americans, who chose to live in Paris because of "a more sympathetic atmosphere."[32] The term, however, was used far more broadly by Read herself and other critics of the day to refer to those who fostered cultural alliances between nations. Bonney was celebrated moderately in the French press, but extensively in the American press during the 1920s and into the 1930s.[33] She was described as an intellectual, a muse for the Parisian avant-garde, an authority on contemporary European art and life, a successful businesswoman and pioneer in the field of international photojournalism, and an emissary of ideas, knowledge, and culture between France and the United States. With the ability to command the attention of the American public through her media connections, Bonney used her fame to promote herself and her business.

Thérèse Bonney achieved attention for her lifestyle and achievements before she became a photographer and successful businesswoman, and was in the early 1920s already gaining celebrity status. The American press began to run stories on Bonney when she was awarded her doctorate from the Sorbonne in 1921. Newspapers hailed her as one of the most academically and intellectually accomplished women of her generation. In 1923, Bonney was included in the *New York Herald* weekly column "Men and Women Who Are Doing Things," where she was noted for "startling French savants" with her insight into the French theater. The column focused on her remarkable academic career and her accomplishments thus far as a translator and adaptor of French plays for the American stage.[34] Because such achievements were indeed rare for a woman during the early twentieth century, they were invariably cited in most subsequent articles about Bonney and were considered to set her apart in her new profession—photojournalism.

Early in her career, she also worked as a fashion model and as an artist's model. An amusing photograph of Bonney posed as Leonardo da Vinci's *Mona Lisa*, by the American expatriate photographer M. Benjamin, appeared alongside many articles.[35] She was also portrayed posing for the painter Robert Delaunay—one such photo accompanied a short piece about Bonney in the *Evening Mail,* in which she tried to dispel the myth

Thérèse Bonney with art dealers Ambroise Vollard (second from left) and Etienne Bignou (far right) on the ocean liner Île-de-France, ca. 1934. Bonney took credit for organizing this first trip to the United States for the modern art dealers, as well as similar trips for various French textile and fashion designers. It was appropriate that they traveled on the Île-de-France, which had been designed by a team of some of the most renowned architects and designers of the day.

of a carefree Parisian life. She warned: "Paris is no place for the ambitious American girl seeking a literary or artistic career—if she cannot speak the French language."[36] A feature on Bonney in the *Evening Telegram* continued along the same vein: "Chances are all against the American girl in Paris. We have the word of Miss Thérèse Bonney, spirited and ultra-intellectual daughter of California, that this is so."[37] Against the odds, Bonney herself had "conquered Paris" through ability and hard work. Hers was the story of a self-made woman—the classic American dream realized abroad.

With the inception of her press service around 1923, Bonney's public persona evolved into a multidimensional entity that she could market commercially and that journalists could promote. Helen Appleton Read's 1924 article in the *Brooklyn Daily Eagle*, entitled "Thérèse Bonney, One of 'The Internationals,'" was one of the earliest features devoted to her. Complete with a photograph of Bonney wearing a fashionable Cubist-inspired ensemble by Sonia Delaunay and subtitled "She Unites France and America Through Her 'Pictures With Ideas,'" this feature encapsulated Thérèse Bonney, the media persona. Bonney deliberately fostered her role and identity as an international—it became her hallmark and ultimately translated into all phases of her career. She even included it on her resumé.[38]

Read's article lauded Bonney's success at interpreting Europe for an American audience. It stated, somewhat reductively, that Bonney supplied "American newspapers and periodicals with photographs of what she selected as the most interesting people and events in Europe."[39] Read considered Bonney's collection to be unique for it included new discoveries, not just established Parisian icons. Read also believed that Bonney's extensive education gave her unequaled authority to select and filter her subject matter.

Read's article, and others that reported on the impact of Bonney's photographs in America and her concern for the spread of information from Europe to the States, not only emphasized Bonney's commitment to her birth country but also suggested her savvy in recognizing the audience she was appealing to. For example, a 1929 article in the *Brooklyn Daily Eagle* claimed that Bonney was "constantly called on by presidents of some of America's largest stores and industries to solve or work out a fashion problem, plan modern decorative or industrial exhibits or an advertising program."[40] This statement may refer to department store Lord & Taylor's landmark "Exposition of Modern French Decorative Art" in 1928, which Bonney claimed to have inspired and

Thérèse Bonney, ca. 1925, in front of the Eiffel Tower. Shortly after arriving in Paris in 1919, Bonney wrote to her mother, "Expect to like Paris—do already." The image of Bonney as a spirited and independent young American in Paris was central to the celebrity she cultivated in the U.S. media.

been involved with. A 1930 feature in *Paris Weekly*, the English edition of *La Semaine à Paris*, portrayed her as a direct conduit for information about the modern movement and confirmed her allegiance to the United States: "Miss Bonney follows the rapid movements of modern art, she picks out its salient points which show at once its advance and its unity. She photographs new furniture, new stuffs and new houses, her articles with their illustrations go to important American reviews and magazines and so the ideas which have been generated in Paris, are spread and explained across the Atlantic."[41]

In the way she manipulated her public image, Bonney typified the twentieth century. As a photographer herself, she realized early on the importance of photographic images in the creation of a public identity. She would always make pictures of herself available to the press, recognizing the advantages of a completely orchestrated presentation. The photographic cult of celebrity of course quickly gained momentum in the twentieth century with the emergence of the Hollywood culture in the 1920s, and still flourishes in the celebrity-obsessed society of today. Moreover, Bonney continually reinvented herself and courted the media for the express purpose of creating familiarity and trust among the American public. In a fiercely competitive industry, she relied on a measure of celebrity in the United States to promote herself and her work. She truly realized that her livelihood, like that of others trying to appeal to a mass audience, depended "upon a numerous and faithful body of admirers."[42] Her public persona, deliberately cultivated, exemplified the twentieth-century "personality" defined by American cultural historian Warren I. Susman. In contrast to the moral implications of the seventeenth-century term "character," Susman argued that "personality" represented more superficial traits, describing one who was "fascinating, stunning, attractive, magnetic, glowing, masterful, creative, dominant, forceful."[43] Bonney's celebrity rested primarily on her exceptional achievements as a woman in the early twentieth century—her academic credentials and her thriving, self-made business in a male-dominated profession. However, it was also fueled by the captivating image of Bonney as an expatriate in Paris—an independent American, free from convention, who socialized with the avant-garde, yet still seemed accessible.

3_parisian design

The vast majority of Thérèse Bonney's formal design photographs were taken in private residences and at annual salons and international expositions. Bonney classified the designers within the modern movement as either "traditionalists" (including cabinetmaker Jacques-Emile Ruhlmann and interior designer Paul Follot, both of whom worked in the Art Deco style) or "out-and-out modernists" (including department store art directors René Prou, head of La Pomone design atelier at Au Bon Marché, and Louis Sognot, of Primavera design atelier at Au Printemps). She believed that the future of the modern movement was in the hands of the latter group, "those who look to this age alone for inspiration, and who find the greatest beauty in a product perfectly adapted to its use. It is among these artists that I believe the decorative art of the age is developing and it is among certain younger ones that I find the most satisfying expressions."[1]

Bonney listed who she regarded as the five most outstanding individuals or ateliers of her day: the interior design firm D.I.M. (Décoration Intérieure Moderne), under the creative direction of René Joubert and Philippe Petit; designer Francis Jourdain; Paul Poiret's design firm Atelier Martine; designer Jean Dunand; and architect Pierre Chareau. Founded in 1914, D.I.M. produced original furniture designs by Joubert and Petit and other domestic furnishings, including rugs, lighting, and fabrics, by a host of designers. Francis Jourdain was one of the first designers in France before World War I to create furniture and objects suitable for mass production; between the wars he

Private homes and salon installations
are the subjects of some of the most important images in the Bonney Service archives. OPPOSITE The spiral staircase in the atelier-home of sculptors Joël and Jan Martel (10, rue Mallet-Stevens), by architect Robert Mallet-Stevens, ca. 1927. The window at right was created in stained glass by Louis Barillet. ABOVE Boudoir designed by Jean Dunand, exhibited at the Salon des Artistes Décorateurs, 1930.

Entrance hall of the Draeger apartment,
designed by Francis Jourdain, with sofa and cabinets of
walnut and wall sconces in translucent glass. Jourdain had
begun his career as a painter, exhibiting with Cézanne,
Matisse, and Toulouse-Lautrec, but had switched to design
in the early 1910s. He designed furniture and interiors and
frequently collaborated with Robert Mallet-Stevens, even
designing interior elements for the architect's own house on
rue Mallet-Stevens, the Paris street named after him.

became one of Robert Mallet-Stevens's most important collaborators. Couturier Paul Poiret founded Atelier Martine, a design firm and art school for girls, in 1911. Through it he produced the students' colorful, naive designs, mostly derived from nature, as textiles and wallpapers. The firm also designed complete interiors. Swiss-born Jean Dunand started his career as a sculptor and went on to become one of the most versatile Art Deco designers in France. Known mainly for his innovative work in lacquer, he designed furniture and decorative objects, collaborated with dressmakers and milliners on clothing and accessories, and created a number of important interiors. Pierre Chareau's work included the design of furniture, lighting, and interiors, as well as architectural commissions, the most celebrated of which was his 1928 glass house for

The D.I.M. showroom and shop (40, rue du Colisée). Bonney considered D.I.M. (Décoration Intérieure Moderne), under the direction of René Joubert and Philippe Petit, one of the most important modern design firms in Paris. OPPOSITE Showroom in the basement of the shop, with nickel tubular railings and white stucco pillars. The built-in sofa had a moveable, pneumatic seat. LEFT Table for phonograph records and studded screen, designed by René Joubert and Philippe Petit, D.I.M. Both pieces were covered in cobalt blue leather.

Geometric floral forms were a common motif in the work of numerous modern designers, from René Prou to Atelier Martine. LEFT Abstracted plant forms cover the pastel-painted walls and floor tiles in this breakfast solarium designed by René Prou and furnished with Marcel Breuer tables and chairs. RIGHT These curtains by Atelier Martine, one of Bonney's favorite studios, feature a bold tropical-print pattern in green for the main curtain and a stylized floral print on the white undercurtain.

Architect and designer Pierre Chareau
worked on a number of important commissions in the 1920s,
including the Maison de Verre, the Paris residence for Jean
and Annie Dalsace, and a renovation of the Grand Hôtel de
Tours in 1928. Bonney called him "ingenious without being
bizarre, intelligent and daring." ABOVE Reading room in the
Grand Hôtel, Tours, ca. 1928, in which Chareau's oak furniture
and alabaster lighting filled the space in tones of brown, silver,
and gold. RIGHT Bonney's portrait of the architect.

Jean and Annie Dalsace in Paris. Bonney reserved her highest praise for Chareau, unabashedly proclaiming him "one of the finest and most sensitive creators of to-day, every year seeing greater responsiveness to the demands of the age."[2] While Bonney regarded all the designers on her list as "out-and-out modernists," her judgment could be idiosyncratic: Jourdain and Chareau were indeed progressive modernists, but Atelier Martine and Dunand generally had a more decorative element in their work.

Chareau's furniture designs were widely favored by other designers. LEFT In the living room of pianist Madame Reifenberg (4–6, rue Mallet-Stevens), by architect Robert Mallet-Stevens, ca. 1927, all the furniture, including rosewood chairs upholstered in brown leather and velvet, was Chareau's. Folding oak panels covered the windows, and sliding oak doors divided living room from dining room. ABOVE Chestnut table (also in rosewood) and lamp in alabaster and silvered metal by Chareau. This photograph was published in *Arts & Decoration*, May 1927.

_private residences

Private houses and apartments, especially those of artists, provided modern designers with a venue for exploring their aesthetic outside of the commercial or institutional realm. Among the private residences that Thérèse Bonney photographed were several inhabited by the artistic and social avant-garde. Bonney's architectural photographs did not typically document entire buildings, inside and out. Rather they were more episodic, as was the case with her photographs of the sleek Paris studio-apartment of the famous Art Deco Polish painter Tamara de Lempicka. This duplex was located at 7, rue Méchain in a building designed by Mallet-Stevens and set back from the street at the end of a courtyard. The apartment itself was also designed by Mallet-Stevens and decorated by him and Lempicka's sister, architect Adrienne Gorska de Montaut, with signature modernist furnishings including metal and built-in furniture. When Bonney photographed the home, she captured the foyer on the first level and the mezzanine library and bar. The foyer contained a modern, nickel-plated metal hall stand and a René Herbst chair of tubular steel and black rubber cords. The library was designed to resemble an ocean liner cabin with a polished walnut built-in sofa and bookcases. The furniture was upholstered in fabric customized with Lempicka's initials.

Interiors by and for well-known Parisians were photographed by Bonney. ABOVE Ship-themed private bar designed by Atelier Martine for the writer Maurice Dekobra (seen in the photograph). Another version of this photo—without Dekobra—was published in *Arts & Decoration*, April 1930. "Famous literary captain takes the wheel," noted Bonney. "Maurice Dekobra, international best-seller, installs latest in bars in his Paris apartment...this corner known as 'La Gondole aux Chimeres' after one of his well-known books. Bar was designed by [Atelier] Martine."

Tamara de Lempicka, the famous Art Deco painter, lived in a studio-apartment at 7, rue Méchain designed in 1929 by Robert Mallet-Stevens and decorated by Mallet-Stevens and Lempicka's sister, Adrienne Gorska de Montaut. OPPOSITE The entrance hall contained a nickel-plated metal hall stand and signature René Herbst chair. LEFT The mezzanine library featured elegant walnut furniture with custom brown and beige upholstery woven with Lempicka's initials.

The home of graphic artist Jean Carlu, designed by Louis Sognot, was bright and open, constructed of clean, simple lines and furnished in a neutral palette of beige and brown. A dramatic staircase and leopard-skin rugs were the only decorative elements to be seen in Bonney's documentation of the space, though the owner's identity is hinted at by an example of his work on an easel. In the house Robert Mallet-Stevens designed for prolific sculptors (and frequent Mallet-Stevens collaborators) Jan and Joël Martel, geometric elements provided both the structure and formal composition. It was precisely these elements that Bonney chose to highlight in her photographs of

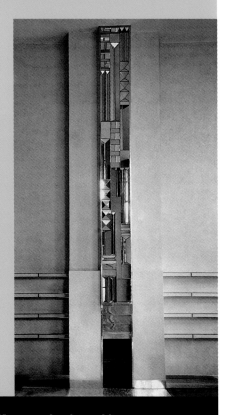

Many modernist architects built atelier-homes for Parisian artists. ABOVE AND RIGHT Details of the home of sculptors Joël and Jan Martel (10, rue Mallet-Stevens), by Robert Mallet-Stevens, ca. 1927. The columnar fireplace of faceted mirror (above) was designed by the Martels. On the terrace (right), key surfaces were clad in brown tile. OPPOSITE Studio-apartment of graphic designer Jean Carlu (17, avenue Carnot), designed by Louis Sognot, ca. 1930.

this famous dwelling. In the roof garden, structural columns doubled as tiered tables. The underside of the home's signature circular watchtower was painted a vivid red. Bonney also focused on the geometric elements inside the property: her photo of the spiral staircase (p.98) is composed as a graphic abstraction.

Bonney photographed both the Paris and Hyères residences of perhaps the most prominent patrons of avant-garde art in Paris in the 1920s and '30s, Vicomte and Vicomtesse Charles and Marie-Laure de Noailles. Their interests extended beyond the fine arts to contemporary film and music, and they subsidized several experimental films created by, among others, Jean Cocteau and Man Ray. Their luxurious Paris home on Place des Etats-Unis, where they frequently entertained the city's artistic elite, was decorated by the young and progressive French designer Jean-Michel Frank. "His rooms for the Comte de Noailles…startle with some unusual features, offset with sober, very elegant furniture," observed Bonney.[3] The grand salon featured massive bronze doors and walls covered in large, rectangular panels of vellum. The spare, unornamented furniture designed by Frank and the rug by American-born designer Evelyn Wyld (a frequent collaborator of designer Eileen Gray) appeared almost slight in the vast space.

The Noailles' villa in Hyères in the south of France was one of Robert Mallet-Stevens' earliest commissions, beginning in 1924. (It was, incidentally, used by the

The Paris and Hyères residences of the prominent art patrons Vicomte and Vicomtesse Charles and Marie-Laure de Noailles. OPPOSITE Corner of the grand salon in their Paris home (11, place des Etats-Unis), by Jean-Michel Frank, ca. 1929. ABOVE Small salon of the Villa de Noailles in Hyères by Robert Mallet-Stevens, 1924–33. A number of other leading avant-garde figures contributed to the villa: the fireplace was by René Prou; furniture and alabaster wall sconces by Pierre Chareau; and printed fabric by Raoul Dufy for Bianchini Férier.

Corner of the salon, Villa de Noailles, Hyères,
by Robert Mallet-Stevens, 1924–33. This room was also
called the "pink room" because the sofas and club chairs were
upholstered in pink rubber. A series of monochromatic stained-
glass skylights by Louis Barillet provided the natural light. The
clock on the far wall, designed by Francis Jourdain, was one of
thirty of the same model used throughout the house.

Noailles' friend Man Ray as the set for his film *Les Mystères du Château du Dé.*)
Interior elements were commissioned from several leading modernists including
Djo-Bourgeois, who created a number of bedrooms; Chareau, who designed an open-
air sleeping room on a terrace; Prou; Jourdain; and Frank. Nonetheless, as captured
by Bonney, elements of the interior—specifically the small salon with overstuffed
chairs and abundant carpeting seeming to crowd the space—appeared less overtly
modern than the Paris residence.

Thérèse Bonney gained entry to many private residences through commissions
for photography from architects and designers. She was hired by Mallet-Stevens, for
example, as early as 1925, and also worked during these years for Pierre Chareau
and Gabriel Guévrékian.[4]

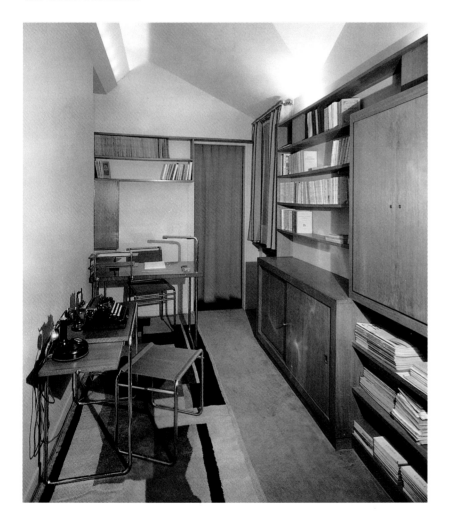

Modern design principles are sometimes more readily
conveyed by photographs of small rather than large spaces.
OPPOSITE Bathroom in Gabriel Guévrékian's apartment for Pierre
Delebart (70, boulevard Flandrin), ca. 1928. Floors and walls
were marble and upper walls silvered metal. The overall effect
was sleek, clinical, and luxurious. LEFT Home office for a private
apartment by French architect Pierre Barbe. Modern details
include Marcel Breuer's tubular steel furniture, built-in bookcases
and cabinets, and a plastic ceiling with concealed lighting.

Duplex living room of Antoine's glass house
(rue Saint-Didier), decorated by Madame Lipska, 1927.
Antoine, a famous Parisian hairdresser, claimed to have
designed the house himself. It took five years to plan and design
and two years to build, and at one point during the construction,
Antoine was the Saint-Gobain glass factory's biggest client.
A bubble-glass staircase led to the balcony seen here, which
was lined with overlapping glass slabs in brilliant red and
Venetian blue. Elsewhere, the overall color scheme was white.

_salons

Artistic salons—special exhibitions presented annually by the professional societies in Paris including the Société des Artistes Décorateurs, the Salon d'Automne, and the Union des Artistes Modernes—played a vital role in introducing modern design to the public in the 1920s and '30s. Most were held at the Grand Palais, and they attracted an international audience with visitors and press coverage from well outside of France.

The Société des Artistes Décorateurs was founded in 1901 to encourage artists and architects working in design to revive the applied arts industries in France and to provide a forum where entire ensembles could be exhibited. Its first salon, held in 1904, was the only one in Paris devoted solely to the decorative arts. World War I forced the suspension of its annual salons between 1915 and 1918, but they resumed in 1919.[5] By the 1920s, the Société's membership included the most notable figures in the field.

The 1926 salon was likely the first Société salon photographed by Bonney. (The 1925 Exposition Internationale des Arts Décoratifs et Industriels Modernes had taken the stage the year before and Bonney had only begun photographing design around 1924.) Within another couple of years, the two main opposing camps of modern design were fully represented in the Société salon. French architect Michel Roux-Spitz's luxurious bath-dressing room for the 1928 salon featured a slightly elevated tub with a monumental banded mirror behind it. The triangular elements in the copper and

The Bonney Service documented the salons of the Société des Artistes Décorateurs, the Salon d'Automne, and the Union des Artistes Modernes. OPPOSITE Bath and dressing room by Michel Roux-Spitz shown at the Salon des Artistes Décorateurs, 1928. LEFT ABOVE Tubular-steel card table and chairs in a smoking room by René Herbst shown at the Salon des Artistes Décorateurs, 1928. ABOVE Burnished copper radiator cover designed by Suzanne Agron that formed part of an installation at the Salon d'Automne.

Department store exhibitions of modern design reached a large and varied audience. Au Printemps installed special signage for its second annual "Petite Foire des Arts Décoratifs Modernes." The tentlike structure with bold, modern typography was clearly designed to conceal the ornate facade of the nineteenth-century building.

aluminum repoussé screen designed by French metalsmith Raymond Subes were echoed in the lower portion of the faceted dressing table and in the glass mosaic floor. The ceiling and wall lighting was designed by Austrian-born lighting designer Jean Perzel in white opaque glass and metal. Roux-Spitz introduced a white bearskin to contrast with the glass and metal in the space. At the modernist end of the spectrum was René Herbst's smoking room almost completely fitted with tubular-steel furniture, with adjoining rooms designed by Charlotte Perriand and Georges Djo-Bourgeois. Bonney captured the section of the smoking room that contained a game table and plush cushioned chairs, the smooth curves of the furniture offset by the strict geometric pattern of the rug.

Representing a stylistic middle-ground in 1928 was French designer Maurice Matet's study (pp.124–25) in which he combined tubular steel with wood and tufted leather upholstery. Created for Le Studium, the decorating department of the Grands Magasins du Louvre, Matet's exhibit was an example of the regular contributions to the salons by the department store design ateliers. Under the direction of some of the era's top designers (Matet, Etienne Kohlmann, and René Prou, among others), these ateliers—including Au Bon Marché's La Pomone, Galeries Lafayette's La Maîtrise, and Au Printemps' Primavera—became a vital force in the modern movement, displaying

The annual artistic salons in Paris presented modern design to a large public. This man's bedroom was designed by Lucie Renaudot for exhibition at the Salon des Artistes Décorateurs. The room's opulent furnishings included white linen sheer curtains with royal blue silk drapes, ebony furniture inlaid with ivory, and brown velvet upholstery.

Woman's study designed by Maurice Matet
for Le Studium, the design atelier of the Grands Magasins
du Louvre department store, shown at the Salon des Artistes
Décorateurs, 1928. Matet combined tubular steel, tufted
leather, and textiles with graphic prints to create
this lively modern environment.

Travel office by Lucie Holt Le Son for the 1929
Salon des Artistes Décorateurs. The upholstery fabric was by
Hélène Henry and the handwoven rug from the Myrbor Gallery.
Modern modes of transport provided the decorative theme of
the room. Holt Le Son, who also designed floor coverings and
other furnishings, was one of a number of female designers in
Paris who were highly regarded by Bonney. She noted that Holt
Le Son was the only American to exhibit at the 1929 salon.

Animal-print textiles and animal-skin rugs were popular decorative elements in Art Deco interiors. ABOVE In this dressing room for an actress designed by Paul Joly for Roumy, the chair and daybed were upholstered in leopard-print fabric. OPPOSITE Zebra-print wool upholstery is a striking element in this office designed by Michel Dufet and created by Au Bûcheron for the Compagnie Royale Asturienne des Mines. Dufet's design was shown at the Salon des Artistes Décorateurs, 1930.

their designs at their own in-store exhibitions and at international expositions in addition to the annual salons. A number of well-known designers created pieces for the department store ateliers, many of them signed. Furthermore, these ateliers engaged in some of the earliest limited serial production of modern design in France.

The 1930 salon of the Société des Artistes Décorateurs was a key moment, for it faced the first salon of the Union des Artistes Modernes, the progressive group of architects and designers that had defected from the Société the year before; the two societies held their salons at virtually the same time. It was also significant because the Société invited the Deutscher Werkbund to exhibit alongside its members, representing the first foreign participation in any of their salons. The Werkbund's contribution, organized by German architect and Bauhaus founding director Walter Gropius, consisted of a boarding house complete with both private apartments and communal spaces, and pieces by, among others, furniture designer Marcel Breuer. The furniture was almost entirely in tubular steel, glass, and metal. It was sober and rational, fully reflective of the machine-age and of the social and cultural ideologies associated with mass production.

The Werkbund's display was vastly dissimilar to the French work that it was shown alongside. Thérèse Bonney captured two particularly compelling installations among the French exhibits, one by designer Michel Dufet, the other by Jean Dunand. Dufet's Art Deco office environment for the 1930 salon achieved a rich, luxurious effect. The focal point of Bonney's photograph was a highly reflective, massive metal desk with red lacquer swivel shelves. The lacquered metal chairs were upholstered in black and white zebra-print wool, while the circular motifs of the desk and stripes of the zebra skin were repeated in the rug. These objects were available through Le Sylve, the design atelier of Au Bûcheron directed by Dufet.

"Among the decorators who have become famous for some particular development, the outstanding is probably Jean Dunand, with his work in lacquer," Bonney observed. "On screens, wall panels, whole walls of rooms, tables, decorative objects, this hard-surfaced, shining medium is modern, completely modern, although its origin is far back in the past."[6] Like Irish-born furniture designer Eileen Gray, Dunand had learned to lacquer under the Japanese artist Seizo Sugawara in Paris, and applied the technique to furniture, screens, wall panels, and beyond. However, Dunand's work tended to be more ornamental than Gray's, employing, for example, Oriental forms that acknowledged the

Salon designed by Hilly for Bernard Rancay,
"one of the young decorating shops of Paris," according
to Bonney. The room was exhibited at the Salon d'Automne.
Curves and circles define the space, from the chairs,
benches, table, and wallpaper motif, to the
distinctive cylindrical chandelier. Offering contrast
are the screen, rug, and polygonal back wall.

ancient origins of the art. His boudoir for the 1930 salon was a fully lacquered space inspired by the exotic. The lacquered furniture, upholstered in suede, was gently sinuous. The round mirror on the dressing table echoed Oriental motifs of giant flowers and water in a lacquer mural that covered an adjacent wall. The three-panel screen, mirrored on the reverse, was lacquered in silver, gold, and black (p.99). Bonney's photograph captured the artistry and nuance of Dunand's work, showing how the curve of the chair legs repeated the folds of the woman's costume on the screen behind.

Another vital exhibition society, the Salon d'Automne, was founded in 1903. Its members also presented annual salons in Paris, with entire ensembles incorporating furniture, objects, painting, and sculpture. From the beginning, it held design in equal standing with the fine arts. For the 1929 Salon d'Automne, Charlotte Perriand, Le Corbusier, and Pierre Jeanneret created a kitchen as part of the interior equipment for a home. Clinical, sleek, and purely functional, it had white cabinets, walls, and floors and steel furniture and fixtures. Bonney photographed the kitchen with its various elements, including the fold-down chopping board and sliding tabletop, in full use. At the same salon, French architect Georges Djo-Bourgeois presented a living room in which he used metal and glass to create a harmonious, functional environment. A horizontal strip of mirrors was inset over the built-in sofa; table and

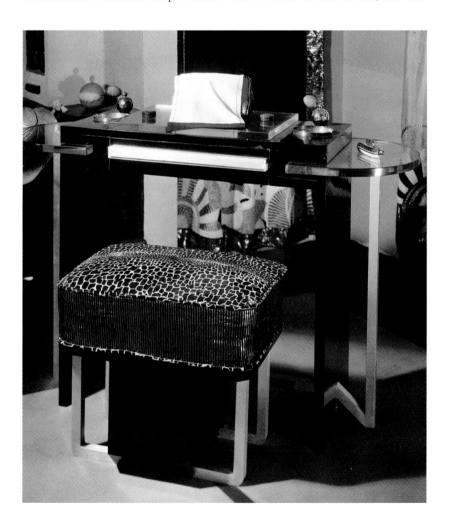

Notable details from salon installations, such as lighting, window treatments, and individual pieces of furniture, were often documented by Bonney. ABOVE Detail of window treatment designed by Mlle. Lebucher in a bedroom designed for a young girl by Saddier for the 1928 Salon d'Automne. The off-white voile sheer curtains were beaded with seed pearls, and the curtains were of rose silk. LEFT Manicure table designed by Alice Courtois.

Kitchen by Charlotte Perriand, Le Corbusier, and Pierre Jeanneret, part of an ensemble of equipment for the home shown at the 1929 Salon d'Automne. In full keeping with the trio's concern with functional, hygienic design, this kitchen featured stainless steel fixtures and utensils, and sleek white cabinets.

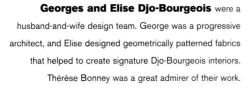

Georges and Elise Djo-Bourgeois were a
husband-and-wife design team. George was a progressive
architect, and Elise designed geometrically patterned fabrics
that helped to create signature Djo-Bourgeois interiors.
Thérèse Bonney was a great admirer of their work.

chair frames were tubular steel; and the printed curtains, designed by his wife and
frequent collaborator Elise Djo-Bourgeois, had a chevron pattern in a muted palette.
"I shall be presumptuous now and say 'Watch Djo-Bourgeois.' A young architect-
decorator, he represents to me the spirit of this age," wrote Bonney confidently. "He
might easily have been a product of America, nourished on its towering smokestacks;
its massive grain elevators; its 'Pacific 231'; its concrete and steel as symbols of speed,
strength and extraordinary adaptation to use and necessity."[7]

Living room designed by Georges Djo-Bourgeois
with chevron-print curtains by Elise Djo-Bourgeois for
the 1929 Salon d'Automne. Around the built-in sofa
was furniture of tubular steel and glass.

Private salon designed by Rémon & fils for the Île-de France ocean liner. The wood paneling of the walls was elaborate. Walnut walls were inset with panels of maple, cedar, and amaranth marquetry. The armchairs were also walnut. Sumptuous browns and greens formed the salon's rich palette. This interior was first exhibited by the Compagnie Générale Transatlantique in the French Pavilion at the 1925 Exposition Internationale des Arts Décoratifs et Industriels Modernes.

_international expositions

Attracting a still broader audience were the three international expositions held in and around Paris in the 1920s and '30s—the 1925 Exposition Internationale des Arts Décoratifs et Industriels Modernes, the 1931 Exposition Internationale Coloniale, and the 1937 Exposition Internationale des Arts et Techniques dans la Vie Moderne. Thérèse Bonney attended and photographed each of them. The 1931 Exposition was a celebration of colonialism, with pavilions from France, Italy, and the United States, among others. The 1937 Exposition presented the work of many of Paris's most important modern architects and designers, and was particularly significant professionally for Thérèse Bonney since it was her last large-scale documentation of modernism.

The 1925 Exposition presented an enormous opportunity to document the Art Deco style at its climax, which the Bonney Service did. However, only a few images of the event exist in the Bonney collection at Cooper-Hewitt, National Design Museum, most of which are clearly identified as the work of other photographers. The Bonney Service caption books confirm that Bonney photographed at least a portion of the fair herself, including Le Corbusier's Pavillon de L'Esprit Nouveau.[8] She also documented Gabriel Guévrékian's small triangular garden of water and light, located on the Esplanade des Invalides. This was enclosed on two sides by triangular glass plaques in tones of red to pink to white. Lush triangular beds of flowers and grass surrounded a fountain composed of four triangular basins on three levels whose interiors were painted by Cubist painter Robert Delaunay with white, red, and blue circles. By night, a spectacular play of color and light was cast over these four basins from a reflective revolving sphere faceted with stained glass and mirror, which was created by French glass designer (and frequent Mallet-Stevens collaborator) Louis Barillet.[9]

In the twelve years between the 1925 Exposition and the 1937 Exposition Internationale des Arts et Techniques dans la Vie Moderne the city of Paris and the design community at large experienced great change. The 1929 New York stock market crash virtually brought an end to luxury design production in France by the 1930s. Paris experienced great unemployment and political upheaval, and by 1937 Europe was on the verge of another war. Despite the high level of design on view at the 1937 Paris fair, politics and economics therefore played an even bigger role than at previous world's fairs. Paul Bastid, French Minister of Commerce, wrote as the fair began:

> World-Depression is retreating. Statistics prove it. Confidence and
> the desire to live and to work must also return to the hearts of men.
> Nations need to stand back and look at their accomplishments in order
> to recover their self-confidence by long years of trials....The message

The monuments of Paris decorate Colette Guéden's "Chic du Chic" ceramic table service. Guéden was director of La Primavera, the design studio of Au Printemps, and created the pattern for the studio's display at the Pavillon des Artistes Décorateurs, part of the 1937 Paris Exposition. Different monuments appeared on different pieces and in different colors—either red, blue, or black, on a white ground.

Glass fountain in the garden of the Pavillon de Saint-Gobain glass manufacturer, designed by architects René Coulon and Jacques Adnet for the 1937 Paris Exposition. Saint-Gobain used glass for every conceivable architectural and interior design element of the pavilion. The theme carried into the garden, where water projected from a glass wall fell into circular glass basins sitting in a shallow pool. The base of the pool was a reflective green and black marmorite mosaic.

of the 1937 Exposition? Peace at home among all Social Classes; peace abroad, good will to nations.[10]

Bastid's essay presented the Exposition as an event that welcomed all social classes, not just an exclusive elite—a vast change from the 1925 Paris fair.

As the 1937 Exposition was mounted, the 1939 New York World's Fair was being planned, and its directors looked to Paris for their model. Though separately organized, the connection between the fairs was inherent—a function of the timing, the themes, and the fact that these host cities were the art and design capitals of the world. There were other significant fairs held elsewhere during these years (including San Francisco's Golden Gate International Exposition in 1939), but those of Paris and New York were firmly aligned by their own organizers, the press, and even the municipal authorities of their respective host cities. In the spring of 1937, New York City Mayor Fiorello La Guardia proclaimed May 2 through May 8 "Paris Exposition Week"—during which time he encouraged New York businesses to participate in the promotion and celebration of the overseas event, no doubt anticipating that the city of Paris would make a similar gesture for the forthcoming New York fair.[11]

The 1939 New York fair opened in even more politically and socially tenuous times than its Paris predecessor, just two years earlier. Europe was once more at war, following Germany's invasion of Poland. The idealistic goal of the long-planned fair, as stated by the fair's Corporation President, Grover Whalen, was to show

the best industrial techniques, social ideas and services, the most
advanced scientific discoveries. And at the same time convey…the picture
of interdependence of man on man, class on class, nation on nation…tell
of the immediate necessity of enlightened and harmonious cooperation
to preserve and save the best of our modern civilization…[and] seek to
achieve orderly progress in a world of peace.[12]

The Bonney family was involved with the New York World's Fair Corporation almost from its inception. The notion of a world's fair in New York had been conceived in the spring of 1935 as a way of improving the poor economic condition of the city—a city, like so many others, trying to recover from the Depression. By the mid-1930s

Louise Bonney was well-known in the field of industrial design in the city and was thus appointed first to the Fair of Tomorrow committee, which was responsible for writing a proposal for the Fair, and then to the Board of Design. Shortly thereafter, in 1936, Thérèse Bonney contacted the organizers with an idea for an exhibit. Although her proposal was not accepted, she was given a contract with the Board of Design and invited to report on the foreign pavilions at the 1937 Paris Exposition Internationale des Arts et Techniques. Specifically, she was to provide the Board of Design with

Gabriel Guévrékian's triangular garden
of water and light, created for the 1925 Exposition Internationale. Often referred to as Guévrékian's "Cubist garden," this comprised triangular beds of flowers and grass, a fountain with triangular basins on stepped levels, and a faceted revolving sphere in stained glass and mirror by glassmaker Louis Barillet. A perforated wall of triangular glass plaques in red, pink, and white enclosed two sides of the garden. Barillet's sphere was illuminated at night.

written descriptions of the various buildings and pavilions, as well as photographs, drawings, and any other material that would be relevant to the design of the New York World's Fair.[13] It was to be modeled closely after the Paris fair, so the detailed information that Thérèse Bonney provided was crucial to their evolving plans.

Architect-critic Henry-Russell Hitchcock and Emily Genauer, editor of the Fine and Decorative Arts sections of the *New York World-Telegram*, each wrote pieces in the press

Dining room in the Pavillon du Louvre, designed by Etienne Kohlmann for the 1937 Paris Exposition. Kohlmann, director of the Le Studium, the design studio of the Grands Magasins du Louvre department store, created the table in glass and white metal, but the seats and backs of the chairs were done in unbreakable heavy plastic. A touch of opulence was added by the gilt spheres on table and chair stretchers and chair backs.

linking the two fairs.[14] Both also accompanied their writings with Bonney photographs—Hitchcock in an article in *Architectural Forum* and Genauer in her 1939 book *Modern Interiors Today and Tomorrow*. Genauer suggested that the "average American" had been introduced to modern design at the 1933 Chicago Century of Progress Exposition, but the modern design on display in New York could be directly credited to the Paris Fair. Her book used Bonney's photographs of mostly French interiors and objects at the Paris Exposition to discuss current European design in relation to American trends. In other words, modern design for a mass audience continued to originate in Europe and be imported in the United States.[15] However, Genauer expressed the belief that the New York World's Fair would shift the center of modern design to the U.S. Curiously, Bonney had predicted the same shift a decade earlier, in 1929: in *A Shopping Guide to Paris* Bonney suggested that by 1940 the United States, where the machine age was already thriving, would lead the world in the creation of modern decorative art.[16] Of course, even in 1939 neither woman could know that the war just begun would severely limit the production of applied arts for the next several years.

The French press also made the link between the New York and Paris Expositions, with Bonney playing a pivotal role. The late 1937–early 1938 edition of the French magazine *Arts et Métiers Graphiques* included a special section devoted entirely to the fairs titled "Expositions Internationales. Paris 1937, New York 1939." Printed in both French and English, it featured articles on many aspects of the Paris Fair. There was just one article about the upcoming New York Fair, written by Bonney, a dry list of facts about location, national and international participation, estimated cost, and special features. However, her photographs of the Paris event appeared throughout the entire issue.

Thérèse Bonney had also held an official role at the Paris Fair, as pictorial consultant to the Franco-American Committee.[17] In this capacity, she photographed all aspects of the event, and was allowed to do so while the site was under construction. It was from this collection that she supplied photographs to both the Board of Design of the New York World's Fair and the press at large. These photographs were also published extensively in the United States throughout the summer and fall of 1937, in the *New York Times*, *Architectural Record*, *Life*, *Arts & Decoration*, and elsewhere.

Indeed the exposition led to a marked resurgence of business for the Bonney Service in the U.S., for Bonney's images seem to have been one of very few thorough documentations of the event.

Bonney's photos and descriptions of the Paris exposition for the New York World's Fair Corporation are also an invaluable and unique record for historians. In the course of her five-month contract, Bonney submitted to the Board of Design well over seven hundred photographs and at least twenty-five reports on the foreign pavilions and French exhibits. Her detailed reports illustrated not only the progress in architecture, technology, and science of the various nations, but also in some cases the political implications of their presentations—the imposing German and Soviet pavilions, situated directly across from each other at the Iena Bridge on the Seine, as seen through Bonney's lens and voice, were especially telling.[18] Germany subsequently withdrew from preparations for the New York World's Fair, in the spring of 1938, and the Soviet pavilion was demolished after the first season—both incidents direct results of the rapidly evolving political crisis in Europe.

Bonney's reports on the Pavillon de la Solidarité designed by Robert Mallet-Stevens and the Pavillon de Saint-Gobain designed by French architects René Coulon and Jacques Adnet in particular reveal her vision of modernism, and her continuing advocacy of the avant-garde and its democratic principles of design. Henry-Russell Hitchcock believed that the Pavillon de la Solidarité "hardly even maintains the level of quality that might be expected of [Mallet-Stevens]," but Thérèse Bonney found it to be one of the most appealing and most modern pavilions at the 1937 Exposition, reflecting both her taste for the rational and austere and her long-time commitment to the work of Mallet-Stevens.[19] Decorated by Maurice Richard, the Pavillon de la Solidarité occupied nearly 11,000 square feet (1,022 m^2). The nine aesthetically distinct rooms of the pavilion presented the evolution and role of public service in France through large photographic prints, photomontage, mural epigraphics, paintings, murals, and charcoal drawings. Sculpture in the pavilion was created by Joël and Jan Martel and Jean Lambert-Rucki. In her report, Bonney paid particular attention to the Propaganda Hall, which featured a blue and white stained glass window symbolizing public service. Twelve paintings, each approximately 6 feet (1.8m) wide and 19 feet (5.8m) tall, were suspended from the ceiling in a circle.

The Pavillon de la Solidarité designed by Robert Mallet-Stevens for the 1937 Paris Exposition. In the exhibition hall hung a photographic montage on the theme of work and its role in society. The doorway to the motion picture room is seen at the end of the hall.

Executed by twelve leading contemporary painters including Fernand Léger, Raoul Dufy, and Jean Lurçat, they "depict[ed] allegorically twelve great organizations of Social Service in France."[20] Bonney found the most outstanding features to be "continuity and co-ordination in presentation, use of color, use of photographic enlargements and charcoal combined, use of art as medium for pictorializing, dramatizing statistics."[21] Her photographs emphasized the architecture and scale of the rooms and displays.

The Propaganda Hall in Mallet-Stevens' Pavillon de la Solidarité was hung with paintings by some of France's most important artists depicting different forms of public service. From left, paintings are by: Fernand Léger, Jacques Le Chevallier, Yves Alix, André Villeboeuf, Jean Souverbie, and Raoul Dufy.

The entrance hall of the Pavillon de la Solidarité,
designed by Robert Mallet-Stevens for the 1937 Paris
Exposition. Seventeenth- and eighteenth-century paintings from
various French museums were displayed in the hall. They were
protected from overexposure to sunlight by a huge panel
suspended from the ceiling. The statue in the foreground is by
Jean Lambert-Rucki, and the charcoal and photographic
montage addresses the themes of deprivation and misery.

PAVILLON
St·GOBAIN
ENTRÉE

In her extensive documentation of the Pavillon de Saint-Gobain, Bonney noted in particular its modern architecture and exhibition technique. One of France's oldest glass manufacturers, Saint-Gobain made their pavilion a showcase for glass as a modern building material. A massive curved glass and steel facade featured stairs constructed of glass slabs supported with concrete, which Bonney described as "impressive and striking."[22] Even the signage—an intertwined S and G monogram with company dates below, designed by the artist Labouret—was made of sparkling silvered glass. On top of the pavilion, "Saint-Gobain" was executed in green neon lights. The remaining walls and ceiling were constructed of glass bricks, while the floors consisted of a combination of glass bricks and glass lenses. Decorative effects, including the veneer for structural columns, were achieved with glass modified to look like marble. A fountain in the garden (p.138) consisted of five glass basins set in a glass mosaic pool. The exhibits, presented in glass and steel cases, told the history of the centuries-old Saint-Gobain glass factory, and included displays of glass lenses and even glass textiles alongside a live demonstration of the glassmaking process. The pavilion masterfully presented a traditional art form in a thoroughly modern idiom.

Thérèse Bonney's involvement with both the 1937 Paris Exposition Internationale des Arts et Techniques and the 1939–40 New York World's Fair represented a turning point in her own career. It marked the end of an era of architectural and design photography for Bonney and was her last major presentation of modern design. It was also an achievement on a truly international scale, for her work inspired, in many ways, the design of the New York World's Fair.

The Pavillon de Saint-Gobain, glass manufacturer, designed by architects René Coulon and Jacques Adnet, for the 1937 Paris Exposition. Glass was used in a great variety of forms and methods throughout. OPPOSITE The stairs to the entrance were glass slabs, the curved front wall was glass and steel, and the Saint-Gobain monogram and dates were executed in sparkling silver glass. ABOVE Inside the pavilion the ceiling, walls, and floor were all constructed of glass bricks. A mirror wall, seen at right, created a brilliant reflective effect.

4_selling modern in the united states

Although she lived in Paris for nearly sixty years, Thérèse Bonney never considered herself an expatriate, for her allegiance always remained with her native country. "I have made my headquarters in France since 1918," she proclaimed, "but I am not an expatriate, I am the dean of the American press corps in Paris. Nobody outdates me."[1] Bonney championed the modern movement in three distinct ways: first, by selling her photographs of contemporary European design to American publications and organizations seeking to publicize a modern aesthetic; second, by positioning herself as an authority on modern French art and life to the American press; and, finally, by writing specifically for an American audience about modern European design and architecture and how it could be emulated in the United States.

_american modern

By the early 1920s Americans were already familiar with the new urban form, the skyscraper, which was universally identified as America's modernist icon. But it was not until the 1925 Exposition Internationale des Arts Décoratifs et Industriels Modernes in Paris that modern design in its various forms was presented on a large scale in the American media. Some previous efforts had in fact been made to acquaint the American public with modern design, including a series of exhibitions by both the Architectural League of New York and the Metropolitan Museum of Art, but the expo-

Modern glassware and ceramics were among a wide range of decorative arts photographed by Bonney. OPPOSITE Glass vase designed by Henri Navarre, who was in Bonney's estimation "a leader in the revival of glassware." In his "way of decorating a vase…bubbles left in the glass itself give a 'frosted' pattern." This photograph was published in *Arts & Decoration*, June 1928. ABOVE Tin-glazed earthenware dish with a reclining bather, designed by Raoul Dufy, ca. 1926 (detail of a photograph showing this alongside a companion piece).

Jean Dunand, one of the most versatile designers
of his era. Best known for his work in lacquer, he also
designed complete interiors as well as sculpture, furniture,
decorative objects, fashion, and jewelry. Bonney praised
the "virility and power...seen in all his work."

sition in Paris gave it a new momentum.[2] The 1925 Exposition was widely advertised
and covered in American art, design, architecture, and fashion periodicals. Coupled
with the media's growing fascination with Paris, this inspired many Americans to travel
to France to see the Exposition themselves. American department stores certainly followed the event closely. The enormous impact that their Parisian counterparts had on
the 1925 Exposition must have suggested the potential for themselves in the States.[3]

The United States declined to participate in the 1925 Paris Exposition because, as
stated by Secretary of Commerce Herbert Hoover, the nation had not yet produced
modern decorative art in any quantity. This prompted curious Americans (led by the
department stores) to look to Europe, mainly France, as a model for the new movement. For those who did not travel to Paris, two exhibitions in the States served as
extensions of the 1925 fair. The first, in October 1925, was a room in the modernist
vein containing textiles, objects, and furniture similar to those exhibited in Paris that
summer arranged by fabric and wallpaper merchants F. Schumacher & Co. in their
New York showroom.[4] The second was a traveling exhibition in 1926 containing
approximately four hundred objects from the Exposition. Opening in Boston, this was
also shown at the Metropolitan Museum of Art in New York, and in Cleveland, Detroit,
Chicago, Minneapolis, St. Louis, Pittsburgh, and Philadelphia. Like the Paris fair in
which it originated, this too was covered extensively in the media.[5]

The success of the two exhibitions, which countless people attended, led to a break-
through in awareness of European design, with department stores taking the lead. By
1926 the major department stores in New York—with Macy's, Wanamaker's, and Lord
& Taylor at the forefront—were selling copies of French modern furniture.[6] And by
1928, Lord & Taylor, for example, had created a department of modern decoration "as
a further step in sponsoring this new art of the 20th century."[7] Lord & Taylor briefly
suggested a new educational role for American department stores when they mounted
their landmark "Exposition of Modern French Decorative Art" in 1928. Featuring furniture and objects designed by such leading modern French designers as Jean Dunand,
Francis Jourdain, and Pierre Chareau, the exhibition was museum-like in both presentation and purpose, since none of the objects on view was for sale.[8] Lord & Taylor's goal
was simply to create a desire for modern design among its customers. The exhibition
deliberately showcased work that represented the spectrum of modern French design

at the time, from the luxurious (Dunand and Jacques-Emile Ruhlmann) to the austere (Jourdain and Hélène Henry). R.H. Macy & Co. followed suit that spring with their "International Exposition of Art in Industry," which featured the work of modern designers not only from France and the U.S., but also from Germany, Italy, Sweden, and Austria.[9]

Bonney claimed to have inspired and collaborated on the 1928 Lord & Taylor show as well as "An Exhibition of Contemporary Decorative Arts" at Marshall Field in Chicago, featuring objects designed by the leading modernists from Europe, though neither catalog credits her efforts.[10] She was also involved with a series of international exhibitions of industrial art organized by the American Federation of Arts in New York. Beginning in 1928, each exhibition focused on one or two media such as ceramics, and traveled to major museums in Chicago, Cleveland, and beyond. Bonney organized the French contribution for a number of these shows.

Despite great strides made by American designers such as Paul Frankl and Donald Deskey, who both promoted an American Art Deco style in the 1920s, stores in the U.S. still frequently dictated a European aesthetic as modernism's ideal. In 1929, the Metropolitan Museum of Art opened its popular exhibition "The Architect and the Industrial Arts," which included only American architects and designers.[11] But this remained exceptional. In general American modern design did not fully come into its own until the early 1930s with the rise of industrial design.[12]

_the written word

From 1925, nearly all American art, design, and decorating magazines, including the usually conservative *House Beautiful* and *House and Garden*, covered the modern movement, often using European examples and an instructive tone. *The Arts* devoted regular columns to modern decorative art in Paris, and in 1926 *The Studio* published a series of features on modern French designers. *Good Furniture Magazine* followed the movement closely and perhaps promoted it more consistently than any other design serial of the period, with not only extensive features on events and topics within the movement, but numerous editorials on the status of modernism in America.[13] Through her writings for various magazines, Bonney was a crucial part of these efforts.

Thérèse Bonney, ca. 1925. Bonney's gray and blue silk crêpe de chine dress is made with Stehli Silks' "My Trip Abroad" print, a detailed map of the streets and monuments of Paris designed by Ralph Barton. Bonney used this photograph frequently for publicity purposes.

Jean Puiforcat and Jean Dunand were two
Parisian designers championed by Bonney. Here, a silver
coffee and tea set with wooden handles, by Puiforcat,
is shown on a woven Rodier tablecloth next to a bronze
and red lacquer vase by Dunand. This photograph illustrated
Bonney's article "New Silhouettes in the French Tea Service,"
published in *Arts & Decoration*, September 1927.

"Madiana Strelya" family of lightweight wools
in pastel shades with black and white French knots designed
by Meyer Frères and chosen by Paul Poiret for one of his
spring collections, photographed alongside a pair of beige
kid gloves designed by Alexandrine.

Besides her series of Paris guidebooks, Bonney wrote a handful of articles on the theme of modernism that were published exclusively in the United States. Like many other journalists and critics, Bonney still looked to Europe as the leader of modern design, but she would soon set herself apart by passionately championing the United States as the place where the movement should flourish. In a September 1927 article in *Arts & Decoration,* "New Silhouettes in the French Tea Service," Bonney highlighted the metalwork of Jean Puiforcat and Gustav Sandoz, the textiles of Paul Rodier, and the lacquered furniture of Jean Dunand. The article also examined the establishment and development of contemporary design in France. Bonney credited the 1925 Exposition as a "tremendous impetus to the modern movement."[14] In these early writings, she still promoted France as the dominant world force in modern design and architecture:

> Paris has not its skyscrapers, but has, on the other hand, an ever-increasing
> number of ultra-modern homes…. The Parisienne…is becoming used to
> the new lines of the modernistic school, she instinctively demands that the
> same spirit repeat itself in the furniture and accessories of her interior.
> Fortunately, there is a new and vigorous movement in Paris, that of the
> decorative arts, in which the best artists and artisans of France are
> employing their talents in modernizing the accessories of the house.[15]

She was sensitive to the general public's wariness about modern design, explaining the modern movement not as a rejection of tradition but as "new forms and formulae when the old have served their usefulness and the times seem to demand fresh interest."[16]

In an article from around 1928 about the avant-garde French designer and gallery owner Madame Myrbor (Marie Cuttoli), she promoted not only the work of Myrbor, but also the modern decor of her salon, designed by French architect André Lurçat, and the modern manner in which she displayed objects. This article was just one part of Bonney's public relations work for Myrbor in the United States.[17] Bonney also organized the first trip to America of modern art dealers Ambroise Vollard and Etienne Bignou in 1934 (p.95). She claimed to have arranged similar trips for textile designers Paul Rodier and Andre Meyer, as well as couturiers Lucien Lelong and Jean Patou, among others. And although she did not extensively document the work

of architect Le Corbusier, she did briefly represent him in America in 1936–37 in the hope of organizing his contribution to the 1939–40 New York World's Fair.[18]

A Shopping Guide to Paris and *Buying Antique and Modern Furniture in Paris*, both published in 1929, served as Bonney's largest single platform from which to discuss her opinion on the state and future of modern design in America. They enabled her to reach the very audience that could effect change—the emerging middle class, and specifically the female consumer.

Nesting tables and fire screen in black lacquer and eggshell, designed by Jean Dunand, and silver tea service by Jean Puiforcat. Dunand used crushed eggshell in his lacquer, and, according to Bonney, raised his own chickens in order to ensure the whitest shells. Of Dunand's lacquer, she wrote, "This hard-surfaced, shining medium is modern, completely modern, although its origin is far back in the past." This photograph was published in *Arts & Decoration*, September 1927.

"Les Dauphins" (the dolphins) wool rug designed
by Jean Lurçat for the Myrbor gallery. Madame Myrbor—
dressmaker, rug designer, and gallery owner—was represented
in the U.S. by Bonney beginning in the late 1920s.

Madame Myrbor (Marie Cuttoli) produced only
five rugs from each artist's design. ABOVE The entrance of
the Myrbor salon (17, rue Vignon), designed by architect
André Lurçat, ca. 1927. On view, from left to right, are
rugs designed by Pablo Picasso, Jean Lurçat, and
Fernand Léger; the rug on the floor was designed
by Lurçat. LEFT Bonney's portrait of Myrbor.

Designs by Paul Rodier and Jean Luce.

OPPOSITE Woven curtain fabric by Rodier, with a metal
lamp designed by Jacques Le Chevallier. This photograph
was published in *Form and Re-Form* by Paul Frankl, 1930.
LEFT ABOVE Sand-engraved vase and bowl with Cubist-
inspired motifs designed by Jean Luce. *Arts & Decoration*
magazine published this image in its June 1928 issue.
LEFT Curtain fabric with fish and wave pattern by Rodier.
ABOVE Paul Rodier (second from left) with, from left, his
nephew Jacques Rodier, nephew Henri Vanier, and son-in-law
Jacques Bignon, 1926.

Tapestry artist Hilda Polsterer in front of
one of her works. Polsterer "introduced a new type of
decorative tapestry," wrote Bonney, with "brilliantly
colored figures painted on fabric...inspired by the
color and people of the African continent."

In the chapter "Modern Decorators," which was included in both books, Bonney anticipated that her observations would rapidly become obsolete since designers and observers in the United States had already begun to acknowledge the movement as a logical extension of their contemporary urban architecture. She wrote:

> Where France leads the way to-day in decorative art, and centers its creations in Paris, possibly another country will lead in 1940. America should since it is here that the machine age, the inspiration for most creative effort to-day, is developing its possibilities.... The resistance to "modern" seems strange, when America goes on expressing itself so straightforwardly in other fields—the simplified skyscraper, the streamline automobile with its elimination of everything except metals and undistorted woods, the bathroom perfectly suited to its use, the sunlit factory. In these creations America has kept abreast of the times, while the home has, for the most part, remained a reflection of the past.[19]

Bonney credited museums, department stores, and designers for the recent advances in American design awareness. She praised Macy's and Lord & Taylor for presenting modern design to the public, Saks Fifth Avenue for their window displays reflecting the machine age, and the small group of American department stores that by 1929 had established contemporary design departments. Bonney, like other critics of the period, felt that modern design principles should encompass not only the objects themselves but the location and manner in which they were displayed. The French, unlike the Americans, were creating complete ensembles and demonstration rooms—an approach considered modern in and of itself. Bonney singled out designer Paul Frankl, architect Eugene Schoen, and journalist Ralph M. Pearson as having made the greatest contributions in promoting American modernism. But she reserved her highest praise for John Cotton Dana, director of the Newark Museum in New Jersey, for breaking new ground in the display of modern decorative art—especially with his exhibitions of industrial art from Germany, beginning in the 1910s.[20]

Just as the 1925 Paris Exposition was a springboard for the dissemination of modern European design, the 1928 inaugural show of the American Designers' Gallery in New

York City was, in Thérèse Bonney's opinion, the first exhibition in the U.S. that approached the same level. A professional association similar to the Société des Artistes Décorateurs and the Union des Artistes Modernes in Paris, the American Designers' Gallery was organized for the purpose of showcasing modern design produced in the United States. In 1928, the American Designers' Gallery exhibited entire rooms created by leading American architects and designers such as Austrian-born Joseph Urban, German-born Weinold Reiss, and Donald Deskey, in addition to single objects by Ruth

A painted tapestry by Hilda Polsterer hangs above the buffet in this dining room featuring rosewood furniture designed by Louis Sognot for Primavera. A glass table and illuminated mirror are visible on the left. Bonney wrote of Sognot and his peers, "Smartness, steadied with simplification, is the keynote of these younger men who pare things down to essentials and still remain provocative." The Bonney sisters included this photograph in *A Shopping Guide to Paris.*

Reeves and Paul Frankl, among many others. This presentation of complete ensembles was certainly among the first in the United States, and after the United States failed to contribute to the 1925 Paris Exposition, the American Designers' Gallery exhibition was a monumental event in American modern design. Bonney concluded the chapter "Modern Decorators" with a polemic, placing responsibility for the future of design in America on her readers' shoulders:

> After your stimulating sightseeing in Paris, you will realize that part of the responsibility in giving America a better place is yours. The artist and the artisan must have an audience. The individual and the community must furnish it. Perhaps you will return with the determination to see that your museum becomes a factor in bridging the gap between the artist and the manufacturer, and the artist and the public, which the machine age makes necessary. And to do your part as a buyer to make the authority of the artist recognized…. America's problem is different, but more stimulating perhaps. We should be creating furniture and homes which can stand proudly beside our skyscrapers, our factories, our airplanes, our automobiles.[21]

The Bonney sisters' Paris books were widely reviewed in the national American press, from *Women's Wear Daily* to the *New York Times*. The reviews were positive across the board. *A Shopping Guide to Paris* was praised as "a comprehensive survey" resulting from "the Bonneys' ten years of experience in the world of styles."[22] *House Beautiful* found that the series "fills a crying need" and the chapter on modern decoration "gives not only an excellent survey of the whole field of decoration, but also practical directions as to where to find and enjoy the work of the most important Parisian artists and decorators."[23]

_marketing the photographs

The Bonney Service's collection steadily acquired renown in the United States from the mid-1920s through the mid-1930s. Charles M. Graves, editor of the Sunday Picture Section of the *New York Times*, wrote to Thérèse Bonney in 1931: "You have built up a distinctive, highly specialized and varied press service…richly chosen, intelligently edited and covering an exceptionally wide range of subjects. It is certainly the outstanding feature service coming out of Europe…. You have brought us the best from these countries."[24]

Each photograph sent out by the service was accompanied by a brief descriptive and sometimes clever caption that provided the name of the designer or architect, the materials and colors used, and the location of the object or interior, almost always including some mention of "modern." Such thoroughness certainly enhanced the editorial usefulness of the photographs in an era when the vibrant colors of Art Deco were not revealed in black and white photography.

Decorating books that featured or at least included examples of modern design were published in increasing numbers in the 1920s and '30s.[25] Bonney's photographs were used in serious design books including Paul Frankl's *New Dimensions* and *Form and Re-Form; Modern Interiors in Europe and America* by Herbert Hoffmann; and *Modern Interiors Today and Tomorrow* by Emily Genauer. Frankl's importance as a designer and tastemaker made his publications particularly influential texts. Born in Austria and trained in both Austria and Germany, Frankl emigrated to the United States in 1914. He was one of the first designers in the U.S. to embrace the modern aesthetic, and designed furniture most notably in the Art Deco style. In addition, he owned the Frankl Galleries in New York, was a founding member of the American Union of Decorative Artists and Craftsmen, and taught modern art at New York University. Frankl's choice to illustrate his books, in part, with Bonney photographs earned her work a sizeable and sophisticated audience.

In *New Dimensions*, which was published in 1928 in the United States, as many as thirty illustrations, or twenty-five percent of the total, could have been Bonney's. (With a few exceptions, the book did not credit illustrations to specific photographers.) Frankl, like other contemporary observers, believed that in the United States modernism found its most common expression in the design of bathrooms. Nonetheless, he illustrated the modern bathroom in *New Dimensions* with four French examples shot by Bonney and presented on two facing pages. Two are of a mosaic-tiled bathroom designed by Raymond Nicolas. The opposite page shows an austere duplex bathroom designed by Gabriel Bouvier. The fourth photograph portrays a dramatic, Art Deco bathtub designed by René Lalique. Frankl repeated Bonney's caption verbatim: "A step

This soaring bathroom by Gabriel Bouvier was designed for the Salon d'Automne, and Bonney's photograph was published in American designer Paul Frankl's *New Dimensions* (1928). Frankl considered the bathroom the most modern room in American homes, but illustrated three French models—photographed by Bonney—in *New Dimensions*. In this green and white marble and tile room, Bonney observed that the "Terraced effect predominates. Note stair treatment, sunken bath and built-in wash bowl illuminated at either side."

towards the glass house…all-glass bathroom created by *Lalique* and exhibited at Salon d'Automne…oval tub in glass reinforced with silver strips…walls in narrow panels of glass."[26] Glass—transparent, hygienic, beautiful—was typically celebrated as an ideal modern building material. The glass house Bonney's caption referred to was itself an important new architectural form. From Bruno Taut's Expressionist glass pavilion at the 1914 Deutscher Werkbund Exhibition in Cologne to the all-glass home built in Paris by Pierre Chareau at the end of the 1920s, glass buildings not only represented the epitome of modern architecture, but also perhaps a utopian vision of design and the built environment.

Frankl also included a number of Bonney photographs in his second book, *Form and Re-Form* of 1930. This volume does credit the photographer of each illustration, so Bonney's contribution is very clear. The chapter in *Form and Re-Form* about textile design, "Weaving," was devoted almost exclusively to Paul Rodier, whose work Bonney often photographed. Accompanying Frankl's extensive discussion were four Bonney photographs of Rodier's geometric woven fabrics. Textile designs by Bonney's friends Raoul Dufy and Ruth Reeves were also included, as were photographs by Edward Steichen and Ralph Steiner that were the basis of prints in Stehli Silks' "Americana" collection. The other Bonney images in *Form and Re-Form* generally portrayed interior ensembles, including a bedroom created by the Parisian design firm Saddier.

Bonney's work consistently appeared in major New York newspapers. She regularly contributed photographs and ideas to a weekly *New York Sun* column for women in the late 1920s and early '30s. One column featured the salon and office of the Parisian dressmaker and milliner Agnès Rittener, known as Madame Agnès. It was illustrated with Thérèse Bonney's photos, and Bonney most likely conceived the story idea as well. The images include three views of the office, designed by Jean Dunand. They captured the angularity of the space, emphasizing the Art Deco style in which Dunand worked.[27] And although Bonney had photographed Madame Agnès numerous times, this article used her photo of Dunand's seductive but androgynous lacquer portrait of Agnès (p.166).[28] The dressmaker's Cubist-inspired clothing, cropped hair, and almost boyish figure complete the picture of a totally modern figure.

American magazines provided still wider exposure for the Bonney Service photographs of design and architecture—trade publications such as *Good Furniture*

Two bathrooms from Frankl's *New Dimensions*.
OPPOSITE Green and blue mosaic tiled bathroom designed by Raymond Nicolas. A second photograph of this room was also included in Frankl's book. ABOVE Oval bathtub of glass and silvered metal created by René Lalique in the Art Deco style. This tub was first exhibited at the annual Salon d'Automne.

Promoting French modernism in the U.S.

ABOVE Collector's study designed by Jacques-Emile Ruhlmann
for the 1926 Salon des Artistes Décorateurs. Jean Dunand's
lacquer portrait of milliner and dressmaker Madame Agnès
(Agnès Rittener) is at the far left. Bonney's photo of this
portrait illustrated a January 1929 *New York Sun* column.
RIGHT Bedroom for a young girl created by the decorating firm
Saddier and shown at the 1928 Salon d'Automne. This image
was published in *Form and Re-Form* by Paul Frankl.

Magazine and *The Gift and Art Shop*, art and design magazines such as *Arts & Decoration*, elite fashion magazines such as *Vogue*, and architecture periodicals such as *Architectural Forum* and *Architectural Record*. Through these magazines, which gave more prominence to photos than newspapers did, Bonney provided a committed audience with vital access to developments in European design.

The Gift and Art Shop was a monthly trade publication for retailers of decorative arts, gifts, and greeting cards, providing information on the latest store display and arrangement techniques. Thérèse Bonney officially joined its staff in May 1929 as manager of the European office—which was, incidentally, her own Paris apartment on rue des Petits Champs, and was featured in the June 1930 issue.[29] Designed by progressive

Thérèse Bonney's own apartment–office
(76, rue des Petits Champs), decorated by Louis Sognot, ca. 1930. OPPOSITE In the small entrance hall, Sognot included a built-in bookcase over the radiator and a cantilevered shelving unit. LEFT A corner of the hall, with furniture by Sognot and Marcel Guillemard. The door and trim were clad in silvered metal. This photo was published in *The Gift and Art Shop*, June 1930. ABOVE The bedroom was furnished with pieces by Pierre Chareau and a brown and beige rug from Myrbor.

French architect Louis Sognot, it was described "as a striking achievement in modern art as applied to interior decoration."[30] The announcement of her appointment touted her as "an internationally known authority on modern art in its relation to the design and styling of merchandise," and continued, "Her pictures and comment will play a valuable part in supplying American retailers of gift and art merchandise with advance information regarding those important trends in design and demand which originate abroad, particularly in Paris, the world's style center, and ultimately and inevitably sway design and demand in this country."[31]

As manager of the European office, Bonney wrote and illustrated a monthly column entitled "As Paris Does It" from 1929 until at least October 1933.[32] Each month she presented a carefully selected group of objects for the home. Although she usually featured small objects such as ceramics, smoking accessories, or lighting, she also showcased furniture and interiors, sometimes devoting the piece to a particular designer or event. The vast majority of her photographs of objects isolated them from any context, thus presenting them as pure design. For a typical column in the August 1929 issue, Bonney wrote about modern jewelry featuring "modernistic, mechanical silhouettes."[33] An accompanying photo portrayed a mannequin's hand dressed with a bracelet and ring by designer Pierre-Yves Mauboussin. Other photographs showed two perfume bottles designed by Paul Beau for Louis Vuitton etched in wheel and cog motifs, a glass desk lamp engraved with a dragon designed by Le Mardele, and silver Hermès cigarette holders. While the perfume bottles were mentioned in the text, the other two images were related only aesthetically.

Another highly illustrated publication to regularly use the Bonney Service photographs was the magazine *Arts & Decoration*. In the September 1929 issue, for example, eight Bonney photographs made up a layout entitled "Wall and Ceiling Lights in French Modernist Effects," featuring lighting by Jean Perzel, Jacques and Jean Adnet, and Pierre Chareau (pp.172–73). Most of these photographs were details of installations at the Salon des Artistes Décorateurs. Bonney photographs appeared frequently in *Arts & Decoration* from 1926 through 1933, and then again in 1937–38.

Good Furniture Magazine used Bonney photographs to actively promote the modern movement. In the June 1929 issue, the piece "Modern Design in Silver" focused on the work of Georg Jensen, Jean Puiforcat, Pierre Colin, and Maurice Daurat and featured

"As Paris Does It" was the title of Bonney's monthly column in *The Gift and Art Shop*. ABOVE The July 1930 column. OPPOSITE Four photos from the August 1929 column. ABOVE LEFT Diamond bracelet and ring by Pierre-Yves Mauboussin displayed on a gray felt mannequin hand designed by Victor-Jean Desmeures for Siégel. ABOVE RIGHT Glass perfume bottles with wheel and cog motif by Paul Beau for Louis Vuitton. BELOW LEFT Engraved glass desk lamp by Le Mardele. BELOW RIGHT Self-ejecting cigarette holder with matching case created by Hermès.

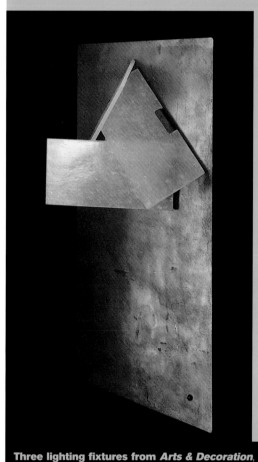

twelve of her photos (pp.174–75). The magazine presented Denmark's Jensen and France's Puiforcat as masters of modernist silver design, although their aesthetics were quite distinct.

Paris was the fashion capital of the world in the 1920s and '30s, and fashion magazines such as *Vogue* and *Harper's Bazaar* were enthralled by it. Not only did many of their articles focus on French fashion, design, and travel, but many of the major Parisian designers and couturiers advertised in their pages. As a result, modern French design assumed an important role within the pages of American *Vogue,* and Thérèse Bonney's photographs were presented in some of these features. Usually they were used in conjunction with the work of other photographers, but one 1930 article titled "Modern French Interiors: Rooms in Neutral Colors" used only Bonney photographs. Featuring interiors by Gabriel Guévrékian, her images emphasized the angularity of their elements, such as the staircase and the fireplace at the Neuilly villa of couturier Jacques Heim.

Although Bonney did consistently document contemporary architecture and major European expositions throughout the 1920s and '30s she preferred to shoot interiors. Consequently her photographs appeared less often in architecture periodicals such as *Architectural Forum* and *Architectural Record.* Only toward the end of the 1930s, with her extensive documentation of the 1937 Paris Exposition, did her work receive significant attention in these magazines. However, her photographs had illustrated some earlier articles, including for example "The Rue Mallet-Stevens, Paris," which appeared in the April 1928 issue of *Architectural Forum.*[34] Composed mainly of photographs and

Three lighting fixtures from *Arts & Decoration*, September 1929. In all, eight Bonney photos illustrated the article "Wall and Ceiling Lights in French Modernist Effects." OPPOSITE Ceiling light by Michel Dufet for Au Bûcheron that demonstrates, as Bonney noted, how "illumination of a room [is] now developed on architectural lines, in which the light fits into the general ensemble." LEFT Trumpet wall light of brown and yellow alabaster and steel, by Jacques and Jean Adnet. ABOVE Forged-iron wall light with alabaster slabs, by Pierre Chareau.

"Modern Design in Silver" in *Good Furniture Magazine*, June 1929, was illustrated with twelve Bonney photos, many of objects exhibited at the 1928 Salon des Artistes Décorateurs. ABOVE Silver flatware with ivory geometric handle detail designed by Pierre Colin for Cardeilhac. RIGHT ABOVE Spiral-handled silver tea service designed by the Danish silversmith Georg Jensen, who opened his Paris shop (239, rue Saint-Honoré) in 1918. RIGHT BELOW Silver coffee service designed by Colin for Cardeilhac.

Rue Mallet-Stevens in Paris is a small residential
street on which all the atelier-houses were designed by architect
Robert Mallet-Stevens, who lived in one of them himself. The
Allatini residence (3–5, rue Mallet-Stevens), ca. 1927, was
designed for a filmmaker and contained a screening room that
held up to 150 guests. This photograph was published in
Architectural Forum, April 1928. (The Cooper-Hewitt print bears
the stamp of both the Bonney Service and photographer Marc
Vaux of Paris, so the shot may not have been by Bonney herself.)

Reifenberg residence, 4–6, rue Mallet-Stevens, by Robert Mallet-Stevens. The narrow four-story stained-glass window was designed by Louis Barillet. This photograph was published in *Architectural Forum*, April 1928. (The back of the Cooper-Hewitt print bears the stamp of both the Bonney Service and photographer Marc Vaux of Paris, so the shot may not have been by Bonney herself.)

architectural plans, this article explored the aesthetics and design philosophy of the modern homes designed by architect Robert Mallet-Stevens on the avant-garde Paris street bearing his name. Bonney's photographs, including those documenting the exterior of pianist Madame Reifenberg's home and that of the filmmaker Allatini, emphasized the many planes and great scale so typical of the street.

_competition

Bonney was not the only photographer, nor her service the only agency, to specialize in modern design in this period. Jean Collas of Paris and Drix Duryea of New York both concentrated on contemporary French interiors and objects. Etablissements Rep ("Rep"), Scaioni, and Sonia—all based in Paris—had vast catalogs of images featuring design, which they sold internationally. The subject matter and aesthetic used by Scaioni and Sonia, in particular, were often very similar to Bonney's.[35] The same American publications that regularly bought Bonney's photos also printed images from these sources. And there were notable American photographers presenting modern American design and architecture to an American audience: Ralph Steiner in *Vogue*, Anton Bruehl in *Vogue* and *Harper's Bazaar*, and Mattie Edwards Hewitt in the *New York Times, Vogue, Arts & Decoration*, as well as a host of art and architecture periodicals. However, Thérèse Bonney alone promoted modernism in more than one medium. None of her competitors wrote articles, curated exhibitions, or represented Parisian artists in New York as she did. Her combined efforts had an unquantifiable but undeniably significant impact on the development of modern design in the United States.

_epilogue

When Thérèse Bonney relinquished her photographic collection to the Cooper Union Museum in the late 1930s, it marked the end of an era for her. The Second World War was to launch a completely new phase in her career as a photojournalist.[1] Nonetheless, her life and achievements continued to be just as remarkable right up until her death in the late 1970s.

She first went to Finland in 1938 to cover preparations for the Olympic games. Upon her return there in 1939, she witnessed and photographed the Russian invasion, images of which were to illustrate her highly acclaimed book, *Europe's Children*, of 1943.[2] She remained in Scandinavia until 1940 and was awarded the White Rose of Finland—the country's highest honor. Bonney then returned to France and covered the Nazi invasion and the Battle of France. She assisted refugees under bombardment at the Belgian border and worked with Anne Morgan's unit of the American Friends of France and again with the American Red Cross. Later in 1940 she traveled to the United States and mounted an exhibition of her photographs at the Library of Congress under the title "To Whom the Wars Are Done." In his foreword to the catalogue, Archibald MacLeish, Librarian of Congress and Pulitzer Prize winner, wrote: "In these quiet and unarguing photographs the people's cause—the one eternal cause which neither force of arms nor fraud of lies can conquer—finds its words."[3] Two hundred photographs from this exhibition were presented in New York at the Museum of Modern Art as "War Comes

Thérèse Bonney photographed by Lee Miller for British *Vogue*, April 1942. This exquisite portrait accompanied a feature on Bonney's wartime career as a photojournalist and her numerous humanitarian initiatives. She was described as a "remarkable woman…[an] intellectual, individual creature; a strong-featured, chunked-out hunk of character."

to the People," and subsequently toured the United States. In 1944, *War Comes to the People* was published as a photo essay in London.

Bonney returned to Europe on a Carnegie Corporation grant in 1941 to document the war's devastation and its impact on civilians. During the war years she also served as a correspondent for *Collier's* magazine and contributed a series of articles to *Vogue* on exiled artists and writers in France including Raoul Dufy and Gertrude Stein. Her photographs of the war and its aftermath had a far-reaching influence. She lectured extensively in the United States about her experiences, and her work inspired the 1948 Academy Award–winning film *The Search*, on which she worked as technical advisor. Starring Montgomery Clift, the film centered on an American soldier in war-torn Germany caring for a young orphan boy as they search for his family at the end of the war. Bonney was even the subject of a comic book titled *Photo Fighter*. In 1945 she personally "adopted" Ammerschwihr, a war-torn French village in Alsace, rebuilding the community and garnering support for its residents. Bonney's extensive chronicle of World War II and her relief efforts proved to be her most publicly celebrated and personally gratifying work. Of her involvement she reflected, "It is hard, hard work—bristling with risks—lucky if you come out of it, but a magnificent chance to contribute your brains and talent to a great cause, the world's—really a privilege."[4] The recipient of numerous French and American governmental honors for her involvement in the war relief effort, Bonney claimed never to have taken pictures again. "I had lived the emotions of the war through the lens. How could I return to commercial photography after that? There was nothing left to take which wouldn't seem trivial."[5]

In 1952, she wrote the official guidebook to the city of Paris, *Paris: Where, What, When, How*, the cover of which was illustrated by her friend Raoul Dufy. She also continued her involvement with numerous humanitarian initiatives in Europe, including establishing the Chaîne d'Amitié, which enabled American G.I.s stationed in France to visit families throughout Europe. In 1964 she was awarded the Grande Médaille d'Honneur de la Ville de Paris. Other projects, mostly unrealized, included a film about Dufy's life and career and a book on the history of photography. In the 1960s, she embarked on a speaking tour of American colleges and resumed efforts to translate American plays for the French stage. By this time, her private collection of art, furniture, and decorative objects from the Art Deco era had earned renown and functioned as a Parisian salon for visiting students and scholars.[6] Among them was the American artist Andy Warhol, a serious collector of Art Deco furnishings, who turned the tables on her and photographed Bonney and her well-appointed apartment.[7]

In the last years of her life Thérèse Bonney lobbied in Washington, D.C., for Medicare benefits for citizens living abroad, she worked toward a degree in gerontology at the Sorbonne, and she began to write her autobiography.[8] She regained some fame in the United States with a few newspaper articles written about her life and career and an exhibition of her photographs of modern design and architecture at the International Center of Photography in New York in 1976. Although she tried to negotiate with her alma mater, the University of California at Berkeley, to provide a house in which she could live surrounded by her extensive art collection and in which she could offer a "seminar-salon" for students, Thérèse Bonney died alone of heart failure at the American Hospital in Paris on 23 January 1978, at the age of eighty-three.[9]

Thérèse Bonney's work in the 1920s and '30s was truly international in scope, with her photographs appearing in some twenty countries worldwide. Nonetheless, the driving motivation behind most all of her initiatives was forging an understanding and alliance between France, her adopted home, and the United States, her homeland. Between the wars, her work centered on the modern movement in Paris, which she passionately documented and championed through her array of professional activities. As an expatriate and a transcontinental businesswoman, she stood apart from other American photojournalists of her generation who shared her goal of promoting the modern movement. She was also marked out by her commitment to modernism not just as an aesthetic but as a way of life. A host of American designers are credited with having made a tangible impact on the proliferation of modernism in the United States; Bonney's role as a conduit and promoter was no less significant, even if it is harder to gauge. Her legacy lives on in her remarkable photographic documentation of interwar Paris—the design, architecture, life, and culture that captivated and inspired observers then and continues to do so today.

La Grande Médaille d'Honneur de la Ville de Paris was presented to Bonney by Jean Aubertin, President of the Conseil Municipal de Paris, on 6 June 1964, at the Musée d'Art Moderne de la Ville de Paris. Bonney's dress, made from Stehli Silks' "My Trip Abroad" print, is one she had worn in the 1920s.

Notes

Introduction pp.8–21

1. *Buying Antique and Modern Furniture in Paris* and *A Guide to the Restaurants of Paris* are complete chapters from *A Shopping Guide to Paris* that the Bonneys published verbatim as separate books.

2. M. Thérèse and Louise Bonney, *A Shopping Guide to Paris* (New York: Robert M. McBride, 1929), 170.

3. The Exposition had been in plan and repeatedly postponed for well over a decade when it was finally realized.

4. Art Deco was embraced, for example, in the United States where it was interpreted by, among others, designers Paul Frankl and Donald Deskey and was popularized in Hollywood films and urban landmarks such as the Chrysler Building and Radio City Music Hall in New York City.

5. The Bauhaus was originally founded to teach design theories and craft traditions.

6. Constructivism and De Stijl were of course important movements in the fine arts as well.

7. Caption for Bonney photograph CFR 029. The broken style and ellipses are Bonney's own.

8. Helen Appleton Read, "Thérèse Bonney, One of the Internationals," *Brooklyn Daily Eagle, Sunday Eagle Magazine* (September 7, 1924), 4.

9. Letter from Thérèse Bonney to Miss Mary Gibson, Curator, Cooper Union Museum, dated May 17, 1937. Smithsonian Institution Archives.

10. There are a number of photographs in the Bonney collection stamped by other photographers but which also read "Please Carry Mention BONNEY." One can only assume these photographs were acquired and used legitimately by Bonney.

Chapter One pp.22–65
Paris between the Wars

1. Program "Commencement Exercises of the College of the Holy Names, Lake Merritt, Oakland, California," June 12, 1913. Archives, Convent of the Holy Names, Los Gatos, California.

2. Letter from Thérèse Bonney to her mother, dated late spring 1917. Unprocessed carton, Thérèse Bonney Papers, The Bancroft Library, University of California, Berkeley.

3. Handwritten list titled "Unforgettable People, Places, Things, Happenings." Unprocessed carton, Thérèse Bonney Papers, The Bancroft Library, University of California, Berkeley.

4. Although the vast majority of the classes she took were in French, she also studied Spanish, English, Latin, Greek, and philosophy. Academic transcript of Mabel Thérèse Bonney, University of California, Berkeley, 1913–16.

5. Evidence that Bonney changed her name in 1916 exists on her academic transcript, University of California, Berkeley, 1913–16. No official public documents before this time include either Teresa or Thérèse. Her birth certificate, in keeping with the practice of the time, included only a last name. Bonney's birth certificate was amended in the 1960s, presumably by Bonney herself, to include the first and second names "Mabel Thérèse." Information regarding her birth certificate was provided by the Bureau of Vital Statistics of Onondaga County, New York.

6. Ron Fimrite, "She's Done Etcetera, Etcetera– Famed Berkeleyan Back for Brief Visit," *Berkeley Daily Gazette* (October 13, 1956), 1.

7. Letter from Thérèse Bonney to her mother, dated late spring 1917. Unprocessed carton, Thérèse Bonney Papers, The Bancroft Library, University of California, Berkeley.

8. Bonney first worked with the American Association of Colleges in 1918 serving as secretary of the reception committee in New York for a group of French students who were to study at American universities. "52 French Girls Here to Bind Nations Closer," *New York Herald* (September 20, 1918), 3.

9. Letter from Thérèse Bonney to her mother, dated May 4, 1919. Unprocessed carton, Thérèse Bonney Papers, The Bancroft Library, University of California, Berkeley.

10. Memorandum from The American Red Cross National Headquarters, dated October 11, 1920. Unprocessed carton, Thérèse Bonney Papers, The Bancroft Library, University of California, Berkeley.

11. Letter from Thérèse Bonney to her mother, dated October 24, 1920. Unprocessed carton, Thérèse Bonney Papers, The Bancroft Library, University of California, Berkeley.

12. Helen Josephy and Mary Margaret McBride, *Paris is a Woman's Town* (New York: Coward-McCann, 1929), 188.

13. Letter from Thérèse Bonney to her family, dated May 11, 1919. Unprocessed carton, Thérèse Bonney Papers, The Bancroft Library, University of California, Berkeley.

14. Bonney's dissertation was titled *Les Idées Morales dans le Théâtre d'Alexandre Dumas Fils*.

15. Letter from Thérèse Bonney to her mother, dated July 19, 1921. Unprocessed carton, Thérèse Bonney Papers, The Bancroft Library, University of California, Berkeley.

16. "Men and Women Who Are Doing Things," *New York Herald* (July 1, 1923), magazine section, 11.

17. Letter from Louise Bonney to Eugene O'Neill, dated September–October 1922. Agnes Boulton Collection of Eugene O'Neill Papers, Beineke Rare Book and Manuscript Library, Yale University.

18. Caption for Bonney photograph GRA 112.

19. My own translation from René Herbst, *Boutiques et Magasins* (Paris: Moreau, 1929).

20. A photograph of La Plaque Tournante at night can be seen in *Architectures de l'électricité* (Paris: Norma, 1992).

21. My own translation from L.P. Sézille, *Devantures de Boutiques* (Paris: Albert Lévy, 1927).

22. Caption for Bonney photograph CSS 009.

23. M. Thérèse and Louise Bonney, *A Shopping Guide to Paris* (New York: Robert M. McBride, 1929), 116.

24. Ibid., 125.

25. Le Grand Écart and Le Boeuf sur le Toit nightclubs were both frequented by Jean Cocteau; the latter took its name from the 1920 pantomime-ballet by Cocteau and composer Darius Milhaud. Billy Klüver and Julie Martin, *Kiki's Paris. Artists and Lovers 1900–1930* (New York: Harry N. Abrams, Inc., 1989.)

26. Nancy J. Troy, *Modernism and the Decorative Arts in France. Art Nouveau to Le Corbusier* (New Haven: Yale University Press, 1991), 208–11.

27. Caption for Bonney photograph IRT 003.

28. Caption for Bonney photograph THT 017.

29. Caption for Bonney photograph SBB 009.

30. Letter from Thérèse Bonney to Miss Mary Gibson, Curator, Cooper Union Museum, dated February 26, 1937. Smithsonian Institution Archives.

31. Russell Lynes, *More Than Meets the Eye: The History and Collections of Cooper-Hewitt Museum. The Smithsonian Institution's National Museum of Design* (New York: Cooper-Hewitt Museum, 1981).

Chapter Two pp.66–97
An American in Paris

1. Thérèse Bonney, Franco-American Curriculum Vitae, ca. 1952, 5.

2. Helen Appleton Read, "Thérèse Bonney, One of the Internationals," *Brooklyn Daily Eagle, Sunday Eagle Magazine* (September 7, 1924), 4.

3. One story states that during a trip to New York she sat for a portrait at the photography studio Underwood and Underwood and was offered a position as assistant to their Paris photographer, and it was through this job that she conceived the idea to start an illustrated press service.

4. Moholy, Henri, and Abbott each did editorial/documentary work while pursuing more expressive work.

5. Julie Davidson, "Wilful queen of the Rotogravure," *The Scotsman* (January 8, 1977).

6. Typewritten report on the activities of the offices M. Thérèse Bonney, dated January 7, 1931. Unprocessed carton, Thérèse Bonney Papers, The Bancroft Library, University of California, Berkeley.

7. In France, for example, her photographs appeared regularly in the magazine *Art et décoration*.

8. In the 1910s Louise Bonney worked as an English teacher in New York City, and like Thérèse, also held a doctoral degree. In 1922 Louise Bonney and a colleague wrote *Handbook for Business Letter Writers* published by Harcourt, Brace and Company. The Bonney sisters' careers seem to have evolved away from teaching simultaneously as they collaborated on theater translations in 1922 and then founded The Bonney Service around 1923. In the mid to late 1930s, Louise married William Leicester, an executive at the Borden Company.

9. Whitney Blausen, "Textiles Designed by Ruth Reeves," unpublished master's thesis (New York: Fashion Institute of Technology, 1992), 73–74.

10. After the World's Fair, Louise Bonney seems to have retired from the field altogether. She had no children and when she died in 1968, Thérèse was left the only remaining member of the family.

11. Marjorie Dorman, "Dr. (Miss) Bonney Reveals How Camera Shots Led to International Career," *Brooklyn Daily Eagle* (May 11, 1929), 2.

12. Addie Bonney became a widow in 1923. Since she lived in New York City and had experience in banking and accounting, the Bonney Service must have seemed a logical partnership for the three Bonney women.

13. "Two Girls and Their Mother Conduct Thriving Business," *New York Telegram* (July 23, 1930), 10.

14. Naomi Rosenblum, *A History of Women Photographers* (New York: Abbeville Press, 1994), 119, 142.

15. October 25, 1973, notarized statement by Arthur Ochs Sulzberger, President and Publisher of the *New York Times*. Carton 12, Thérèse Bonney Papers, The Bancroft Library, University of California, Berkeley.

16. Dilys Blum, Curator of Costume and Textiles at the Philadelphia Museum of Art, pointed out Bonney's documentation of Schiaparelli's collections.

17. M. Thérèse and Louise Bonney, *A Shopping Guide to Paris* (New York: Robert M. McBride, 1929), 250.

18. Ibid., 247.

19. Caption for Bonney photograph ILV 048.

20. M. Thérèse and Louise Bonney, *A Shopping Guide to Paris*, 73.

21. Caption for Bonney photograph SSS 020.

22. Caption for Bonney photograph STS 060.

23. This information was provided by Betty Kirke.

24. Elsa Schiaparelli, *Shocking Life* (New York: E. P. Dutton, 1954), 164. Schiaparelli continues, "They had uncommon self-effacement, a touching modesty, great love and dedication to what then seemed to many a lost case—France!"

25. Axel Madsen, *Sonia Delaunay. Artist of the Lost Generation* (New York: McGraw Hill, 1989), 255.

26. Bonney photographed Jean Lurçat and his work; Lurçat painted Bonney's portrait in 1933, rendered a plaster bust of her, and gave her his first tapestry design, which was embroidered by his mother. Bonney extensively photographed Pierre Chareau's work, including his famous Maison de Verre, designed in collaboration with Dutch architect Bernard Bijvoët, for Jean and Annie Dalsace on rue Saint-Guillaume, while under construction in the late 1920s.

27. Jean-François Pinchon, editor, *Rob. Mallet-Stevens: Architecture, Furniture, Interior Design* (Cambridge, Massachusetts: MIT Press, 1990).

28. *Mallet-Stevens. Dix Années de Réalisations en Architecture et Décoration* (Paris: Ch. Massin, 1930).

29. In preparation for her unrealized autobiography, Bonney compiled a list titled "Friends" on which some of the above mentioned are included. Unprocessed carton, Thérèse Bonney Papers, The Bancroft Library, University of California, Berkeley. This information was confirmed and/or supported by various other sources.

30. Julie Davidson "Wilful queen of the Rotogravure," *The Scotsman* (January 8, 1977), 6.

31. Letter from Anne Morgan to Thérèse Bonney, dated May 10, 1934. Unprocessed carton, Thérèse Bonney Papers, The Bancroft Library, University of California, Berkeley.

32. Helen Appleton Read, "Thérèse Bonney, One of The Internationals," *Brooklyn Daily Eagle, Sunday Eagle Magazine* (September 7, 1924), 4.

33. Although Bonney appeared occasionally in newspapers throughout the country including the *San Francisco Chronicle*, most of her coverage appeared in the major New York newspapers which would have reached a proportionately large percentage of Americans. The population of the United States around 1930 was estimated at 120 million and the population of New York State 12 million. Of those living in New York State an estimated 10,522,000 lived in urban areas. United States Bureau of the Census, *The Statistical History of the United States From Colonial Times to the Present* (New York: Basic Books, 1976), 9, 32.

34. "Men and Women Who Are Doing Things," *New York Herald*, (July 1, 1923), magazine section, 11.

35. See, for example, "An American model 'Mona Lisa' as portrayed by the camera," *New York Herald* (May 20, 1923), rotographic section. According to William Overend in his 1967 feature on Bonney, this photograph hung in her apartment, alongside portraits of her by such modern masters as Georges Rouault, Robert Delaunay, and Raoul Dufy, suggesting the importance she placed on this element of her career or at least on this particular image. William Overend, "An Extraordinary Expatriate," *International Herald Tribune–Washington Post* (January 24, 1967).

36. "New York Girl Back from Paris," *Evening Mail* (January 10, 1924), 2.

37. Jane Dixon, "Ultra Intellectual California Beauty Urges Invader of France to Stop, Look and Listen," *Evening Telegram* (January 13, 1924), 6.

38. Bonney supported this statement in her C.V. with a number of testimonials extracted from letters and articles about her.

39. Helen Appleton Read, "Thérèse Bonney, One of The Internationals," *Brooklyn Daily Eagle, Sunday Eagle Magazine* (September 7, 1924), 4.

40. Marjorie Dorman, "Dr. (Miss) Bonney Reveals How Camera Shots Led To International Career," *Brooklyn Daily Eagle* (May 11, 1929), 2.

41. Emma Cabire, "A Lover of France. Miss Thérèse Bonney," *Paris Weekly* (February 14–21, 1930), 38–39.

42. As quoted from Herbert Croly, *The Promise of American Life* (New York: Macmillan, 1909), in Warren I. Susman, "'Personality' and the Making of Twentieth-Century Culture" in *Culture as History: The Transformation of American Society in the Twentieth Century* (New York: Pantheon Books, 1984), 281.

43. Warren I. Susman, "'Personality' and the Making of Twentieth-Century Culture" in *Culture as History: The Transformation of American Society in the Twentieth Century* (New York: Pantheon Books, 1984), 277.

Chapter Three pp.98–147
Parisian Design

1. M. Thérèse and Louise Bonney, *A Shopping Guide to Paris* (New York: Robert M. McBride, 1929), 173–74.

2. Ibid., 183.

3. Ibid., 187.

4. The Bonney Service account books. Unprocessed carton, Thérèse Bonney Papers, The Bancroft Library, University of California, Berkeley.

5. Yvonne Brunhammer and Suzanne Tise, *French Decorative Art 1900–1942. The Société des Artistes Décorateurs* (Paris: Flammarion, 1990).

6. M. Thérèse and Louise Bonney, *A Shopping Guide to Paris*, 189.

7. Ibid., 186.

8. The Bonney Service caption books at Cooper-Hewitt, National Design Museum contain duplicates of Bonney's typewritten captions—one book contains captions for photographs listed alphabetically by designer; another, captions for photographs listed by Bonney's own numerical system.

9. The triangular garden of water and light served as the model for Guévrékian's 1927 Cubist garden at the Villa de Noailles in Hyères. For further discussion on both gardens see Dorothée Imbert, *The Modernist Garden in France* (New Haven and London: Yale University Press, 1993) and Élisabeth Vitou, Dominique Deshoulières, and Hubert Jeanneau, *Gabriel Guévrékian 1900–1970, une autre architecture moderne* (Paris: Connivences, 1987).

10. M. Paul Bastid, "The Message of the 1937 Exposition," *Exposition Paris 1937. Arts Crafts Sciences in Modern Life* (May 1937), 5.

11. Memo dated April 21, 1937. Box 254, Folder PR, New York World's Fair, 1939, Inc., and 1940, Inc. Records, The New York Public Library Manuscripts and Archives Division.

12. New York World's Fair 1939, Incorporated, *Official Guide Book of the New York World's Fair 1939* (New York, 1939), 5.

13. For the initial contract she was to be paid a total of five hundred dollars, in three disbursements, which included expenses such as travel to and from the exposition to her home in Paris, postage and secretarial assistance; and she was to be reimbursed, up to two hundred dollars, for the cost of photographs and other reproductions. Bonney was to send these materials directly to the World's Fair New York office in the Empire State Building, but was also to send copies of correspondence and other written materials to John Hartigan at the World's Fair Paris office at 79 Champs-Elysées. It was through Hartigan that she was to be paid for her work. May 22, 1937, contract between T. Bonney and the New York World's Fair Board of Design, written and signed by Stephen F. Voorhees. Box 8, Folder A1.13, New York World's Fair, 1939, Inc., and 1940, Inc. Records, The New York Public Library Manuscripts and Archives Division.

14. Genauer also wrote a number of books on the fine arts and won a Pulitzer Prize in Journalism in 1974.

15. With regard to the Paris Exposition, Genauer first manifested this idea in a 1937 article about the Fair. She believed that the American Pavilion was wholly inadequate and that other smaller nations did a much better job of aligning arts and techniques within their pavilions and exhibits, regardless of the fact that the United States was leading the world in technology. Emily Genauer, "All-Star Cast," *Parnassus* (October 1937).

16. M. Thérèse and Louise Bonney, *A Shopping Guide to Paris*, 169.

17. April 2, 1937, letter from T. Bonney to Grover Whalen. Box 254, Folder PR, New York World's Fair, 1939, Inc., and 1940, Inc. Records, The New York Public Library Manuscripts and Archives Division.

18. Bonney's reports are located in the New York World's Fair, 1939, Inc., and 1940, Inc. Records, The New York Public Library Manuscripts and Archives Division.

19. Henry-Russell Hitchcock, "Paris 1937," *Architectural Forum* (September 1937), 162.

20. June 12, 1937 report on the Pavillon de la Solidarité, 1937 Paris Exposition. Box 255, Folder PR, New York World's Fair, 1939, Inc., and 1940, Inc. Records, The New York Public Library Manuscripts and Archives Division.

21. Ibid.

22. Caption for Bonney photograph #856 of the Pavillon de Saint-Gobain 1937 Paris International Exposition. Box 545, Folder Saint-Gobain Pavilion, New York World's Fair, 1939, Inc., and 1940, Inc. Records, The New York Public Library Manuscripts and Archives Division.

Chapter Four pp.148–79

Selling Modern in the United States

1. Nan Robertson, "In a Life of Firsts, She Has Few Regrets," *New York Times* (July 25, 1976), 38.

2. For a thorough discussion of these and other exhibitions of architecture and design before and after 1925 in New York, see "Exhibitions" in Robert A. M. Stern, Gregory Gilmartin, and Thomas Mellins, *New York 1930: Architecture and Urbanism Between the Two World Wars* (New York: Rizzoli International Publications, 1987), 329–55.

3. The pavilions of the design departments of the four leading French department stores—Primavera (Au Printemps), La Maîtrise (Galeries Lafayette), Le Studium (Grands Magasins du Louvre), and La Pomone (Au Bon Marché)—were given central locations at the 1925 fair, impressing upon the visitor the importance of these businesses and the significance of their design. See Nancy J. Troy, *Modernism and the Decorative Arts in France. Art Nouveau to Le Corbusier* (New Haven: Yale University Press, 1991).

4. Robert A.M. Stern et al., *New York 1930*, 331.

5. For example, an article in the *American Magazine of Art* about the installation at the Metropolitan Museum of Art commented that "the collection in New York was shown beautifully and awakened a great deal of not only curiosity but genuine interest." "Modern Decorative Arts from Paris at The Metropolitan Museum of Art," *American Magazine of Art* (April 1926), 174.

6. Robert A.M. Stern et al., *New York 1930*, 336.

7. The staff of Lord & Taylor's department of modern decoration exhibited five rooms of their design at the "Exposition of Modern French Decorative Art." Advertisement for Lord & Taylor's "Exposition of Modern French Decorative Art" in *Vogue* (March 1, 1928).

8. In an advertisement for the exposition, Lord & Taylor listed as participants: Jacques-Emile Ruhlmann, (Louis) Süe et (André) Mare, Vera Choukhaeff, D.I.M., Rodier, Bianchini Férier, Hélène Henry, Madame Cuttoli of Myrbor, and Lucien Vogel, in addition to Chareau, Dunand, and Jourdain.

9. The American rooms were designed by Kem Weber, William Lescaze, and Eugene Schoen; the Italian rooms by Gio Ponti and Felice Casorati; the German rooms by Bruno Paul; the Austrian rooms by Josef Hoffmann; and the French rooms by Jules-Emile Leleu, Maurice Dufrene, and René Joubert and Philippe Petit (D.I.M.). Each of the six participating countries also had numerous exhibitors in the various decorative arts including furniture, ceramics, rugs, and glass.

10. The catalog for the Lord & Taylor exposition was written by Helen Appleton Read, who had written a favorable 1924 feature on Bonney for the *Brooklyn Daily Eagle*. This previous connection goes some way to validate Bonney's claim to have been involved with the exhibition. Evidence of Read authoring the catalog was found only in Robert A.M. Stern et al., *New York 1930*, 337.

11. Of the exhibition Helen Appleton Read wrote, "Unquestionably the record-breaking crowds which the exhibition has brought forth, necessitating its extension through the summer months, are to be accounted for beyond a mere display of curiosity. These new arrangements are bound up with the changing point of view of the times; they touch something of fundamental importance. New needs, new standards of taste are forming and fermenting; useless conventions and habits of living, at one time believed to be essential for the proper maintenance of a household, are being discarded. Already, even before the creative intelligence of the architect and designer entered in, a new style was inevitably forming in answer to these needs and tastes." Helen Appleton Read, "The Architect and the Industrial Arts," *Bulletin of the Metropolitan Museum of Art* (May 1929), 147.

12. Among those who created modern design in the United States before 1930, in addition to Frankl and Deskey, were Hungarian-born Ilonka Karasz, Finnish-born Eliel Saarinen, German-born Kem Weber, and Walter von Nessen, also of Germany. Stehli Silks' "Americana" dress silks were also an important early example of American modern design.

13. In 1930 the magazine was renamed *Good Furniture and Decoration*.

14. M. Thérèse Bonney, "New Silhouettes in the French Tea Service," *Arts & Decoration* (September 1927), 96.

15. Ibid., 50.

16. Ibid., 96.

17. M. Thérèse Bonney, "Mme. Myrbor Creates True Ultra-Modern Ensemble in Her Art Fashion Salons in Paris," undated newspaper clipping ca. 1928. Carton 13, Thérèse Bonney Papers, The Bancroft Library, University of California, Berkeley. The Mybor Gallery was well known for producing handwoven rugs with designs by artists such as Jean Lurçat, Fernand Léger, and Pablo Picasso.

18. Correspondence between Thérèse Bonney and Le Corbusier, 1936–37. Fondation Le Corbusier, Paris. Claire Bonney pointed to this correspondence in her article "Focus on modern living: Thérèse Bonney's record of Paris moderne" in *docomomo*, Journal 14 (November 1995), 47.

19. M. Thérèse and Louise Bonney, *A Shopping Guide to Paris*, 169–70.

20. In continuing her discussion of the efforts made by American museums in the 1920s she credited those made by the Brooklyn Museum and the Metropolitan Museum of Art.

21. M. Thérèse and Louise Bonney, *A Shopping Guide to Paris*, 208–9.

22. "Experts Here Aid Tourists To Find Bargains in Paris," *The World* (May 12, 1929), 5N.

23. M.A.N., untitled book review of *A Shopping Guide to Paris* by M. Thérèse and Louise Bonney, *House Beautiful* (July 1929), 28.

24. In his letter to Bonney, Graves went on: "I consider that you have been an important factor in the development of closer relations between Europe and America and especially in interpreting France to your own people." Letter dated December 9, 1931, from Charles M. Graves, Editor, Sunday Picture Section, *The New York Times*, to Thérèse Bonney. Portfolio Book, Thérèse Bonney Papers, The Bancroft Library, University of California, Berkeley.

25. Among such publications were *The New Interior Decoration* by Dorothy Todd and Raymond Mortimer of 1929, *The Study of Interior Decoration* by Alice and Bettina Jackson of 1928, and *Modern French Decoration* by Katharine Morrison Kahle of 1930.

26. Caption for Bonney photograph INB 006.

27. A number of fashion designers in Paris embraced the Art Deco style in their salons and homes, including Jacques Doucet and Jeanne Lanvin.

28. A Bonney photograph of Agnès taken at the 1925 Paris Exposition, for example, is in the collection of the Bibliothèque Historique de la Ville de Paris.

29. Beginning with the October 1930 issue of *The Gift and Art Shop*, Bonney consistently invited readers to visit her "office" on rue des Petits Champs. Likewise, Thérèse and Louise Bonney invited readers of *A Shopping Guide to Paris* to visit the office-apartment.

30. "In 'The Gift and Art Shop's' New Paris Office," *The Gift and Art Shop* (June 1930), 19.

31. "Thérèse Bonney Joins Us," *The Gift and Art Shop* (May 1929), 14.

32. Beginning in March 1932 the column was called "As They Do It In Paris." In the 1930s, Bonney's photographs also illustrated other writers' articles in *The Gift and Art Shop*.

33. M. Thérèse Bonney, "As Paris Does It," *The Gift and Art Shop* (August 1929), 17.

34. On the first page of this article, Bonney's name was mistakenly spelled "Bouney" in the photo credit. Two of the five photographs are located in the Thérèse Bonney Photograph Archive at Cooper-Hewitt, National Design Museum. Not uncommonly, Bonney's stamp was placed over that of photographer Marc Vaux of Paris. Whether she had permission or not, Bonney clearly sold these photographs to *Architectural Forum* as her own.

35. The work of Scaioni appeared regularly in *Harper's Bazaar*; the work of Sonia appeared regularly in American *Vogue*.

Epilogue   pp.180–83

1. Although her last extensive body of work in the field of design appears to be her documentation of the 1937 Paris Exposition Internationale des Arts et Techniques dans la Vie Moderne, the New York Public Library has some Bonney photographs of the French Pavilion at the 1939–40 New York World's Fair.

2. In her curriculum vitae, Bonney claims the founding of UNICEF was inspired by *Europe's Children*.

3. Invitation to the opening of "An Exhibition of Photographs by Miss Thérèse Bonney," Library of Congress, November 15, 1940. New York Public Library.

4. "Bonney, (Mabel) Thérèse," *Current Biography 1944* (New York: H.W. Wilson, 1944), 53.

5. Julie Davidson, "Wilful Queen of the Rotogravure," *The Scotsman* (January 9, 1977).

6. Thérèse Bonney Papers, The Bancroft Library, University of California, Berkeley. Highlights from her collection, now housed at the Berkeley Art Museum, include works by Raoul Dufy, Georges Rouault, Robert Delaunay, and Jean Lurçat; furniture by Pierre Chareau; and rugs, including one designed by Fernand Léger, from Myrbor.

7. This information was provided by William Burke.

8. Bonney did not complete her autobiography before her death, so it was never published.

9. Andrea Fraser and the University Art Museum, University of California at Berkeley, *Aren't they lovely? An exhibition of the bequest of Thérèse Bonney, Class of 1916* (Berkeley: University Art Museum, University of California at Berkeley, 1992), exh. cat., 4.

Select Bibliography

Arwas, Victor. *Art Deco*. New York: Harry N. Abrams, 1992.

Barré-Despond, Arlette. *Union des Artistes Modernes*. Paris: Editions du Regard, 1986.

Bonney, M.T. "New York World's Fair 1939," *Arts et Métiers Graphiques* (1937/1938).

Bonney, M. Thérèse. "New Silhouettes in the French Tea Service," *Arts & Decoration* (September 1927).

——. "Mme. Myrbor Creates True Ultra-Modern Ensemble in Her Art Fashion Salons in Paris," Undated newspaper clipping, circa 1928. Thérèse Bonney Papers, Bancroft Library, University of California, Berkeley.

——. *Remember When. A Pictorial Chronicle of the Turn of the Century and of the Days Known as Edwardian…From the Collection of M. Thérèse Bonney*. New York: Coward McCann, 1933.

——. *The Vatican*. Boston: Houghton Mifflin, 1939.

Bonney, M. Thérèse, and Louise Bonney. *A Shopping Guide to Paris*. New York: Robert M. McBride, 1929.

——. *Buying Antique and Modern Furniture in Paris*. New York: Robert M. McBride, 1929.

——. *A Guide to the Restaurants of Paris*. New York: Robert M. McBride, 1929.

——. *French Cooking for American Kitchens*. New York: Robert M. McBride, 1929.

——. *French Cooking for English Kitchens*. London: G. Allen & Unwin, 1930.

"Bonney, (Mabel) Thérèse," *Current Biography 1944*. New York: H.W. Wilson, 1944.

Bonney, Thérèse. *Europe's Children 1939 to 1943*. United States: self-published, 1943.

——. *War Comes to the People*. London: Pendock Press, 1944.

Brunhammer, Yvonne, and Suzanne Tise. *French Decorative Art 1900–1942: The Société des Artistes Décorateurs*. Paris: Flammarion, 1990.

Byars, Mel. *The Design Encyclopedia*. New York: John Wiley & Sons, 1994.

Cabire, Emma. "A Lover of France. Miss Thérèse Bonney," *Paris Weekly* (February 14–21, 1930).

Davidson, Julie. "Wilful queen of the Rotogravure," *The Scotsman* (January 8, 1977).

Davies, Karen. *At Home in Manhattan. Modern Decorative Arts, 1925 to the Depression*. New Haven: Yale University Art Gallery, 1983.

Dorman, Marjorie. "Dr. (Miss) Bonney Reveals How Camera Shots Led To International Career," *Brooklyn Daily Eagle* (11 May 1929).

Duncan, Alastair. *Art Deco Furniture: the French Designers*. London and New York: Thames & Hudson, 1992.

Exposition Internationale des Arts Décoratifs et Industriels Modernes. *Encyclopédie des Arts Décoratifs et Industriels Modernes au XXième Siècle: twelve volumes documenting the Paris exhibition of 1925*. New York: Garland, 1977.

Frankl, Paul T. *New Dimensions: The Decorative Arts of Today in Words and Pictures*. New York: Brewer & Warren, 1928.

——. *Form and Re-Form: A Practical Handbook of Modern Interiors*. New York: Harper & Brothers, 1930.

Fraser, Andrea. *Aren't they lovely? An exhibition of the bequest of Thérèse Bonney, Class of 1916* [exh. cat., University Art Museum, University of California at Berkeley.] Berkeley, 1992.

Genauer, Emily. *Modern Interiors Today and Tomorrow: A Critical Analysis of Trends in Contemporary Decoration as Seen at the Paris Exposition of Arts and Techniques*

and Reflected at the New York World's
Fair. New York: Illustrated Editions Company,
1939.

Herbst, René. Boutiques et Magasins. Paris:
Moreau, 1929.

Hiesinger, Kathryn B., and George H. Marcus.
Landmarks of Twentieth-Century Design:
An Illustrated Handbook. New York: Abbeville
Press, 1993.

Hitchcock, Henry-Russell, Jr. "Paris 1937,"
Architectural Forum (September 1937).

———. "Paris and Flushing: Sober Thoughts on
Twentieth Century Expositions," Shelter
(April 1938).

Hoffmann, Herbert. Modern Interiors in Europe
and America. London: The Studio Limited,
1930.

Hooper, Parker Morse. "The Rue Mallet-Stevens,
Paris," Architectural Forum (April 1928).

"In the Gift and Art Shop's New Paris Office,"
Gift and Art Shop (June 1930).

Joël et Jan Martel, sculpteurs 1896–1966.
Paris: Gallimard/Electa, 1996.

Josephy, Helen, and Mary Margaret McBride.
Paris Is a Woman's Town. New York:
Coward-McCann, 1929.

Klüver, Billy, and Julie Martin. Kiki's Paris:
Artists and Lovers 1900–1930. New York:
Harry N. Abrams, 1989.

Levi, Julian Clarence. "The Paris Model for the
Fair," American Architect (February 1936).

Lord & Taylor. An Exposition of Modern French
Decorative Art [exh. cat., Lord & Taylor.]
New York, 1928.

Mallet-Stevens. Dix Années de Réalisations
en Architecture et Décoration. Paris: Ch.
Massin, 1930.

Mann, Carol. Paris Between the Wars. New York:
Vendome Press, 1996.

Marcilhac, Félix. Jean Dunand: His Life and Works.
New York: Harry N. Abrams, 1991.

Metropolitan Museum of Art. The Architect and the
Industrial Arts. An Exhibition of Contemporary
American Design [exh. cat., Metropolitan
Museum of Art.] New York, 1929.

"A Modernist, One of the Most Successful
Designers of Paris, Works in an Atmosphere
in Harmony With Her Ideas," New York Sun
(January 29, 1929).

Musée des Arts Décoratifs. Les Années UAM,
1929–1958. Paris: Union des Arts Décoratifs,
1988.

Overend, William. "An Extraordinary Expatriate,"
International Herald Tribune–Washington Post
(January 24, 1967).

Pinchon, Jean-François, editor. Rob. Mallet-
Stevens. Architecture, Furniture, Interior Design.
Cambridge, Massachusetts: MIT Press, 1990.

Read, Helen Appleton. "Thérèse Bonney, One
of 'The Internationals,'" Brooklyn Daily Eagle,
Sunday Eagle Magazine (September 7, 1924).

"Recherches et Compositions D'Artistes
Américains Pour La Décoration des Étoffes,"
L'Illustration (March 6, 1926).

R.H. Macy & Co. An International Exposition
of Art in Industry [exh. cat., R.H. Macy & Co.]
New York, 1928.

Rosenblum, Naomi. A History of Women
Photographers. New York: Abbeville Press,
1994.

Sézille, L.P. Devantures de Boutiques. Paris:
Albert Lévy, 1929.

Stern, Robert A.M., Gregory Gilmartin, and Thomas
Mellins. New York 1930: Architecture and
Urbanism Between the Two World Wars. New
York: Rizzoli International Publications, 1987.

Street, Julian. Where Paris Dines. Garden City,
New York: Doubleday, Doran & Company, 1929.

Susman, Warren I. "'Personality' and the Making
of Twentieth-Century Culture," in Culture as
History: The Transformation of American
Society in the Twentieth Century. New York:
Pantheon Books, 1984.

"Thérèse Bonney Joins Us," Gift and Art Shop
(May 1929).

Thérèse Bonney, une americaine. Thérèse Bonney
Photograph Archive, Cooper-Hewitt, National
Design Museum, Smithsonian Institution, circa
1950.

Troy, Nancy. Modernism and the Decorative Arts
in France. Art Nouveau to Le Corbusier. New
Haven: Yale University Press, 1991.

"Two Girls and Their Mother Conduct Thriving
Business," New York Telegram (July 23, 1930).

Vitou, Élisabeth, Dominique Deshoulières,
and Hubert Jeanneau. Gabriel Guévrékian
1900–1970, une autre architecture moderne.
Paris: Connivences, 1987.

Photography Credits

All photographs from the collection of
Cooper-Hewitt, National Design Museum
(with copy photography by Matt Flynn), except:

Courtesy University of California, Berkeley
Art Museum
pages 24, 68 (right)

The New York Public Library, Photography
Collection, Miriam and Ira D. Wallach Division
of Art, Prints & Photographs. Astor, Lenox, and
Tilden Foundations
pages 50–51, 53, 88, 96, 171 (SIBL branch)

Courtesy Bibliothèque Historique de la Ville
de Paris
pages 64, 65, 137, 140, 142–47, 159 (right)

Courtesy University of California, Berkeley
Bancroft Library
pages 89, 90–91, 95, 106 (right), 134 (left and
right), 150, 183

The New York Public Library, Manuscript
and Archives Division, New York World's Fair
(1939–1940) Records
page 138

L'Illustration (March 6, 1926)
page 151

Photograph by Lee Miller © Lee Miller Archives,
Chiddingly, England
page 180

Acknowledgments

Researching the life and work of Thérèse Bonney for the past five years has been an incredible journey. Many kind and generous people along the way have enriched my life and work, and without their assistance this project would not have been possible. I have made every attempt to ensure that all of the information in this book is both factual and correct. Any errors contained within are solely my own.

At Cooper-Hewitt, National Design Museum, Smithsonian Institution in New York I must thank Susan Yelavich, former Assistant Director for Public Programs, for the opportunity to write this book and for her helpful comments on the manuscript; Paul Warwick Thompson, Director, for his support of the project; Jeff McCartney, former Contracting Officer, for his long-time commitment to a project on Thérèse Bonney; Lindsay Staṃm Shapiro, Head of Exhibitions, for her own early work on Thérèse Bonney and for her insightful suggestions to the manuscript; Stephen Van Dyk, Chief Librarian, for his wisdom, humor, and friendship, and for allowing me complete access to the Bonney photographs; the entire library staff; Mel Byars for cataloging Cooper-Hewitt's Bonney photos and making them usable; Jill Bloomer, Image Rights and Reproductions; photographer Matt Flynn; and finally my editor, Elizabeth Johnson, for her sound management of this project and her careful and intelligent edits, which have made this book much more than I hoped it could be. The Andrew W. Mellon Foundation Endowment has also supported my research. At the Smithsonian Institution Archives in Washington, D.C., Bruce Kirby uncovered vital information that would have otherwise been missed.

A major source of my research was Thérèse Bonney's manuscripts at the Bancroft Library, University of California, Berkeley. My gratitude goes to Anthony Bliss, Curator of Rare Books and Manuscript Collections; Jack von Euw, Curator of Pictorial Collections; and William Roberts, University Archivist. I extend a special thanks to David Kessler whose interest in and assistance with my research has been profuse. He is simply a researcher's dream. At the Berkeley Art Museum, University of California, Lisa Calden, Collection and Exhibition Administrator, and Cheryl Maslin, Rights and Reproductions, were particularly helpful. I must also thank Sister Madeleine Rita Murphy, Archivist, California Province, Convent of the Holy Names, and Sister Ethel Mary Tinneman, College of the Holy Names, California, for helping me to reconstruct Bonney's early years in California.

Another important source of my research was the collection of Bonney photographs and the New York World's Fair 1939–1940 Records at the New York Public Library. I wish to thank Sharon Frost, Photography Specialist, for allowing me access to the Bonney collection and the staff of the Manuscripts and Archives Division for their assistance with the Fair Records. I am also grateful to Phyllis Ross for first pointing out the Bonney family involvement in the fair.

Librarians and archivists in farflung places helped me to locate relevant documents. I thank Kathy Kraft, Radcliffe Archives, and the staff at the Schlesinger Library at Radcliffe College, Cambridge, Massachusetts; the staff of the Beinecke Rare Book and Manuscript Library at Yale University, New Haven, Connecticut; Arabella Hayes at the Lee Miller Archive, East Sussex, England; and Debra Clark, Registrar, at the Bureau of Vital Statistics of Onondaga County, New York, for her help in piecing together the Bonney family history in New York State.

In Paris, I must thank Liza Daum, Département des Photographies, Bibliothèque Historique de la Ville de Paris, who allowed me access to the Thérèse Bonney photographs in their collection, and who spent so much time and shared so much of her insight with me. I thank the staff at the Agence Photographique, Caisse Nationale des Monuments Historiques et des Sites, for assistance in reviewing their collection of Bonney photographs. I appreciate the help of Evelyn Trehin, Director, and the library staff of the Fondation Le Corbusier. I also thank Suzanne Tise for sharing her knowledge; Mary Blume for her insight and her recollections of Thérèse Bonney; and finally William Burke for his interest in my work, for many wonderful conversations, and for his own vivid recollections of Bonney. More than anyone, he brought Thérèse Bonney to life for me.

I am particularly grateful to Beverly Brannan, Curator of Photography, Prints and Photographs Division, Library of Congress, for sharing so much knowledge and information. Her generosity inspires awe. My thanks are due to Dilys Blum, Curator of Costume and Textiles, Philadelphia Museum of Art, for her insight on Bonney's fashion photography. In New York, J. Stewart Johnson, Consultant for Modern Design and Architecture, Metropolitan Museum of Art, shared his recollections and materials on Bonney, and Betty Kirke offered her own memories of Bonney. I also thank Claire Bonney Brüllmann in Switzerland.

Many friends have also been vital in the realization of this book. I wish to thank Dr. Maria Ann Conelli for her encouragement and advice and her strong support of my work; Dr. Mary Beth Betts for her early mentorship of my work on Thérèse Bonney; Jeni L. Sandberg for first introducing me to the Bonney photos at Cooper-Hewitt, National Design Museum; Eva Schwartz for her insightful edits of the manuscript; Corinne and René Facchetti for their wonderful translations; Lina Srivastava for her legal counsel; Lourdes Font; Wendell Hafner; Leslie and Geoff Oblak; Marilyn Lawrence; Erica Chase-Salerno; Amy Weinstein; and finally my dear friend Bridget Colman for her unflagging interest and encouragement, her vital research assistance, and for simply always understanding.

Lastly, I wish to acknowledge my family, to whom I dedicate this book. I thank my parents, Richard and Ellen Schlansker, for their generosity and the many opportunities that led me to this place, for providing a sanctuary where I could write, and for giving their time so selflessly this past year. I simply could not have written this book without their help. I thank my brother, Richard Schlansker, for his deep friendship. And finally, I thank my husband, David Kolosek, for allowing Thérèse Bonney to be a part of our lives for the past five years, for his love, sacrifices, great patience, and for never once allowing me to think I couldn't accomplish this; and my daughter, Ella, for inspiring me every single day.

Index